Consumption in an Age of Information

Edited by
SANDE COHEN
and
R. L. RUTSKY

Oxford • New York

First published in 2005 by

Berg

Editorial offices:

1st Floor, Angel Court, 81 St Clements Street, Oxford OX4 1AW , UK

175 Fifth Avenue, New York, NY 10010, USA

Berg is the imprint of Oxford International Publishers Ltd.

Library of Congress Cataloging-in-Publication Data

Consumption in an age of information / edited by Sande Cohen and R.L. Rutsky.

    p. cm.

    Includes bibliographical references and index.

    ISBN 1-84520-089-6 (pbk.) — ISBN 1-84520-088-8 (cloth)

   1. Consumption (Economics)—Social aspects. 2. Information society—Economic

aspects. 3. Information technology—Economic aspects. 4. Consumer behavior. I. Cohen, Sande.

II. Rutsky, R. L.

    HC79.C6C674 2005

    306.3'09'051—dc22

    2005017083

British Library Cataloguing-in-Publication Data

A catalogue record for this book is available from the British Library.

ISBN-13 978 1 84520 088 6 (Cloth)
  ISBN-10 1 84520 088 8 (Cloth)

    ISBN-13 978 1 84520 089 3 (Paper)
    ISBN-10 1 84520 089 6 (Paper)

Typeset by JS Typesetting Ltd, Porthcawl, Mid Glamorgan.

Printed in the United Kingdom by Biddles Ltd, King's Lynn.

www.bergpublishers.com

Consumption in an Age of Information

Contents

Contributors

Jean Baudrillard is the author of many books and a seminal thinker in postwar Critical Theory. His provocative notions of simulation and sign-value, among others, are ubiquitous in contemporary criticism.

Sande Cohen is the author of the forthcoming *History Out of Joint* (Johns Hopkins, 2005), and co-editor of *French Theory in America* (Routledge, 2001), as well as other books and essays in historical theory and cultural criticism. He teaches in the School of Critical Studies, CalArts.

Sean Cubitt is Professor of Screen and Media Studies at the University of Waikato. He is the author of, among other works, *Digital Aesthetics* (1998), *Simulation and Social Theory* (2001), and *EcoMedia* (2005); and co-editor of *Aliens R Us: Postcolonial Science Fiction* (with Ziauddin Sardar) (2002) and *The Third Text Reader* (with Rasheed Araeen and Ziauddin Sardar) (2002).

Sylvère Lotringer is Professor of French at Columbia University. Co-founder of the journal *Semiotext(e)*, he has been instrumental in making the work of French writers available in the USA. He is the author of *Overexposed* (1988) and numerous books and essays.

Tom Lutz is Professor of English at the University of Iowa. He is the author of *Cosmopolitan Vistas* (2004), *American Nervousness – 1903* (1991), and *Crying: A Natural History of Tears* (1999).

Mark Poster is Professor of History and Film and Media Studies at UC Irvine. He is the author of, among numerous books, *The Mode of Information*

(1990), *The Second Media Age* (1995), *Cultural History and Postmodernity* (1997), and *What's the Matter with the Internet?* (2001).

R. L. Rutsky teaches in the Cinema Department at San Francisco State University and is the author of *High Techne: Art and Technology from the Machine Aesthetic to the Posthuman* (1999), and co-editor of *Strategies for Theory: From Marx to Madonna* (2003) and *Film Analysis: A Norton Reader* (2005).

Samuel Weber is Avalon Foundation Professor of Humanities at North-western University. He is the author of numerous books, among which are *Theatricality as Medium* (2005), *Institution and Interpretation* (2001/1987), *The Legend of Freud* (2000/1982), and *Mass Mediauras: Form Technics, Media* (1996).

James Wiltgen teaches Latin American cinema and history in the School of Critical Studies at CalArts.

Introduction: Consumption in an Age of Information

Sande Cohen and R. L. Rutsky

A thesis in many accounts of the contemporary world is that an economic, technological, and cultural shift has occurred: from production to reproduction, modern to postmodern, monopoly capitalism to late capitalism, cultural mediation to cultural immediacies, industrial to informational technologies. Many of these accounts also depict this change as a movement, or shift in emphasis, from production-based practices to consumption-oriented practices. It is perhaps not coincidental, then, that the increasing role of consumption has coincided with the rising precedence accorded to concepts – and practices – of digitization and information. Information and consumption have become dominant practices in the world, not only in "Western" societies, but in many areas of the "non-Western" world, from Shanghai to Rio to Singapore.

As ever larger parts of global experience have come to be seen as "data," information has become the very currency of consumption. We no longer suffer simply from the weight of history, as Marx suggested, but from the burden of an ever-increasing density of information. Indeed, as the quantity of information available for consumption has increased, so have the number of "top-ten" and "best of" lists, "buying guides," "idiot's guides," "FAQs," and similar meta-texts offered to help us navigate the time-space of information. These meta-texts serve as handy how-to guides for the successful consumption of information. In an age of information, then, consumption has increasingly become a matter of meta-consumption. We constantly find ourselves consuming information that summarizes, overviews, or tells us how to find other information that we might wish to consume.

This practice of meta-consumption is certainly not limited to the "commercial" world; it also applies to the so-called realms of knowledge. In academic discourse, where every "secondary source" is by definition information about other sources of information, meta-consumption is a time-honored practice. Anthologies, too, are another meta-textual means by which information on a topic can be filtered, collected, and presented for consumption. This is certainly the case with the present volume, which aims to provide, if not exactly a summary, then at least a highly interdisciplinary overview of the ubiquitous role of consumption within the context of contemporary information and media society. Yet, any book about consumption – and certainly one about consumption and information – is inevitably a form of meta-consumption. Even as it examines consumption, it is itself an object of consumption, something to be consumed. In this, it is symptomatic of an important change that has taken place in the conditions – and conceptions – of consumption. In an age of information, it has become increasingly difficult to distinguish the consumption of knowledge from the consumption of information, and of culture more generally. Watching a film, browsing a web page, or reading a book has become as much a matter of information consumption as buying a product. As this volume cannot help but demonstrate, then, consumption can no longer be considered simply as an object of analysis, held at a distance by a critical view; it is also something in which we – as readers and as critics – inevitably participate.

In an age when media and information technologies raise new questions about what it means to "consume," understanding our changing relation to consumption requires a re-examination of the often unstated assumptions that underlie our views of consumption. While much has been written about consumption, consumers, and consumer society, the vast majority of this work has taken the idea of consumption for granted, as an a priori category. Consumption remains undeveloped as a complex relation. Some works (e.g. economic theories of consumption such as Milton Friedman's) have sought to explain consumer behavior, while other work has aimed to chart the history and growth of consumer society (e.g. the work of Stuart Ewen). Numerous studies have presumed to critique the practices of consumption, from the Frankfurt School's discussion of "the culture industry" to more recent explorations of consumerism such as George Ritzer's *The McDonaldization Thesis* (1998). Yet, in these discussions of consumers and consumerism, the concept of consumption has remained largely unexamined, with rare exceptions (e.g. the work of Georges Bataille on excess Jean Baudrillard's interrogation of need, consumption, and production and Zygmunt Bauman's emphasis on performance as an alternative to production/consumption).

The situation has been somewhat different among theorists of information and computer technologies. Many writers (Stewart Brand and John Perry Barlow, among others) have pointed out that information differs from material commodities such as food or fuel, inasmuch as it is not "used up" in being consumed. Yet, strangely, these writers have not, for the most part, seriously pursued the larger cultural and political implications of this change in the status of consumption. To the extent that they have addressed the social issues of information consumption, they have almost invariably focused on issues of "accessibility" to information – thus assuming that consumption is an undisputed societal goal, and that any problems associated with it are merely a matter of enabling a more equitable (or "democratic") consumption.

In our view, then, the key schools that have traditionally provided a basis for interpreting consumption – from Marxist theory (the Frankfurt School and others) to neo-liberalism (visibly present in the writings of Thomas Friedman of the *New York Times*) to neo-conservativism (associated with formations such as the Chicago School) – have not processed or brought out the changed conditions of cultural production, distribution, and consumption.

These schools have, first of all, generally tended to define consumption as a matter of material accumulation – a view that was already suspect, as Jean Baudrillard pointed out years ago, but which has become largely nonsensical in a world where consumption is less a matter of material goods than of signs and information. An equally problematic issue is that in each of these approaches, consumption is almost invariably conceived in opposition to production, often with the implication that consumption is a passive counterpart to the activity of production. Yet, in an age of information, this distinction, too, seems increasingly anachronistic, as the production of information becomes increasingly subordinated to its reproduction, which often occurs at the level of distribution and consumption, not in its conditions of production. A similar distinction has often been made, particularly in cultural criticism, between consumption and use. As Marxist cultural critic Raymond Williams once argued, "The fundamental choice that emerges, in the problems set to us by modern industrial production, is between man as consumer and man as user" (Williams, 1980). The essence of this distinction between user and consumer is the idea that consumption is merely concerned with imaginary or ideological desires, while use is supposed to be a matter of actual, concrete needs. Yet, as even Marx himself recognized, use value and needs are to some degree culturally determined. Somewhat more radically, Baudrillard, whose outstanding early work on consumption is now too often ignored, has critiqued the very notions of production, need, and utility, which in his view are themselves ideological *effects* of the capitalist system of exchange. For Baudrillard, in fact, consumption – which he sees less as a matter of material exchange than as a circulation of images, signs, and simulation – is the primary force in contemporary societies. This is all the more the case – as Baudrillard himself acknowledges in his interview with Sylvère Lotringer in this volume – in an age of information.

In reconsidering what constitutes consumption as we move into an age of information, this volume attempts to bring work on consumption into productive confrontation with studies of media and information. In this regard, an underlying premise of this volume is that the concepts and practices involved in information and consumption are themselves active forces of social transformation. The essays in *Consumption in an Age of Information* therefore explore – through different methods of analysis and intellectual starting-points – how both consumption and information have begun to transform one another. From "smart homes" to the role of "speed" in contemporary culture to the re-canonization of contemporary art, from downloading MP3 files to the ritual qualities of consumption, these essays examine how, in an increasingly information-oriented world, our conceptions and practices of consumption have – in ways that we are not always fully aware of – begun to change.

The volume opens with a discussion between Jean Baudrillard and Sylvère Lotringer, conducted in Paris in 2004. As Lotringer points out, Baudrillard has been one of the most provocative analysts of consumption for more than thirty years. Baudrillard's views of information and consumption are again provocative here. No one highlights the strange paradoxes of society and history better than Baudrillard. Returning to a longstanding issue, he considers what have variously been called "epistemic shifts" or "paradigm ruptures," in which notions of origin and goal are tossed into the air. To think of information and consumption in terms of historical concepts such as progress and decline is to weave together data and fictional narratives. But it is not just that Baudrillard continues the line of thought that says destruction makes history. Rather, here he turns to the metahistorical. As the codes and rules of social organization now shift from simulation to information technologies more directly, the sign is killed off, subsystem by subsystem. The sign was the anchor for the labor of simulacra building – signs allowed for the play of difference and distinction, even if in the end they were absorbed by simulations that relocated reality as a series of sign-values, among Baudrillard's most notable conceptual offerings. The murder of the sign tells us that we live with an "immediation of things." We move, unevenly, toward an "immaterial fetishism which is that of information." Humanism and its utopias offer rearguard responses while academics and artists have actually become part of the larger schizo-scene.

Following Lotringer's discussion with Baudrillard, we have grouped the essays by Mark Poster, Tom Lutz, and R. L. Rutsky, focusing on the theme of redefining consumption and its highly networked relations with culture. Mark Poster's essay begins by probing the slippage between the literary form of science fiction and actual technological conquests. If the condition for producing science fiction was its telling of the possible, the imagination of the unimaginable, then what to make of the conditions in which the possible is more firmly lodged in "humamachines" than in literature or culture, generally? Focusing on the writings of Philip K. Dick, Poster is curious if the current form of advertising isn't very like what Dick called forth – a culture thoroughly shaped by mediated information. Has advertising become a form that organizes thought? If so, if advertising as such comes to reinforce new social hierarchies, and gives a spiritual value to the selling of commodities, then what remains of both public life and privacy, the latter subject to invasion?

Thomas Lutz's essay, "Spending Time," takes up issues of how we relate today to the multiple times that we inhabit. Ironically considering Benjamin Franklin's brutal reduction that time = money, Lutz discusses subjective movement stretched between leisure or self-assigned tasks and our senses of clock-time that keep us riveted to obligations. Noting that it is difficult in contemporary American academic life to sustain life and work in multiple temporalities, Lutz is skeptical toward an identity he sees between "postmodern and premodern time [that] privilege the timeless," postmodern standing in for the present-as-eternal and premodern for cyclical rituals. To those senses of time, he offers "non-synchronic, multiple, incommensurable yet coexisting layers of time", which have to be struggled for in everyday life. R. L. Rutsky's essay revisits Stewart Brand's famous maxim, "information wants to be free," as a means of understanding information in relation to consumption. In the course of this examination, which points to the role that consumption plays within information, Rutsky argues that this maxim would more appropriately be revised to read, "information wants to be consumed." Thus, Rutsky suggests that the movements of both information and consumption are less a matter of exchange than of dissemination or diffusion, which commodity capitalism always attempts to turn in a (circular) circulation, capable of yielding a "return."

The four essays grouped in the second part take up information and consumption less from the perspective of consumption and more from the perspective of grappling with what we are, collectively, becoming in terms of information as consumed. Sean Cubitt's essay strenuously argues that no monocausal theory can put together relations between clients, agency, medium, and audience. Of course, instrumental knowledge is "in hock to capital," as he puts it, but the media is also, he insists, a "market in attention." Audience attention adds value to programs, channels, and portals. Between the media and society stands the divisions of audiencing, the latter "either as social entities engaged in appropriating media or as economic agents translating media into social actions." Information cannot be separated from "attention-value," which complements and differs from a labor theory of value as well as from Baudrillard's notion of sign-value (which, as said above, is fast disappearing). For Cubitt, each audience is itself a mediation, moving between "entropy, homeostasis, and emergence." Hence, audience consumption is not some enormous graveyard of used-up things, but in various ways a production of information – which allows us to conceive of a responsible "citizen of a media democracy." The optimism of Cubitt and the "objective irony" of Baudrillard make an interesting contrast.

James Wiltgen's essay starts from Foucault's notion of a disciplinary society and the pressures that transform it, asking what becomes of the human subject once technologies begin to suggest such practices as "downloading consciousness." As information becomes increasingly disembodied, what becomes of the subject's will to power? As we become objects of a domination that we have ourselves enacted, who is in control? In answer, Wiltgen outlines what he terms sado-monetarism, which occurs when markets take the place of religion (forming an interesting overlap with Weber's essay on religion and capitalism). Yet, at the same time, he advances a new concept of digital markets, which are understood as a conjunction of utilitarianism and ressentiment – where use-value becomes abuse-value – thoroughly mixed with one another. Digital capitalism brings an endless oscillation between boredom (for the consumer) and uncertainty since capital functions via an axiomatics of immanence.

Samuel Weber's essay employs some ideas from Walter Benjamin, arguing for the relevance Benjamin drew between capitalism and religion. Weber stresses that present capitalism is indeed a cult of the unmediated – an "immediacy of the cult" – or is the autonomous source of meaning "without truce or grace." The appeal to "bare life" through debt-as-guilt fuses capital and religiosity, capital an "unremitting guilt-producing cult" because with it subjective distress comes to know survival-as-life. In fashion, for instance, death and debt are built-in as theatrics of the self. In this, the ideal of knowledge as information without responsibility to past or to future furthers such processes as cultural and political targeting, the very antithesis of imaginative thought that can only "tread," as Weber puts it, in the world.

Finally, Sande Cohen's essay asks about the place and functions available to cultural-political criticism in a social order determined by disparities or disjunctions between information and consumption. Discussing notions raised by Lyotard, Deleuze and Guattari, and Baudrillard, Cohen examines how both scientific practices and aesthetic strategies today are enmeshed in competitive processes that have changed the rules of awarding cultural credit and cultural status. In Cohen's view, disjunctions of information and consumption – as in extensive remedialization of the arts and humanities that nonetheless require "avant-garde" knowledge – require terms for criticism. But it is not clear what to expect from criticism when it has been decontextualized. As knowledge is now the subject of the stories we tell, as we are buffeted by information subject to ratios of frequency and redundancy, as new patterns of control emerge, traditional ideas of cultural-political criticism are threatened with soft extinction, as when book reviewing is reduced to book-promoting.

REFERENCES

Ritzer, George (1998), *The McDonaldization Theses: Explorations and Extensions.* London; Thousand Oaks, CA.: Sage Publications.
Williams, Raymond (1980), "Advertising: the Magic System," in *Problems in Materialism and Culture: Selected Essays.* London: Verso, pp. 170–95.

CHAPTER I

The Murder of the Sign

Jean Baudrillard

SYLVÈRE LOTRINGER: You were one of the first to demonstrate that the logic of consumption did not rely on the acquisition of objects, but on a manipulation of signs. Far from responding to some system of needs, the object only exists as an exchange-value – caught up in an incessant process of sign differentiation.

JEAN BAUDRILLARD: This is what I would call the passage to sign-value. Consumption is a system of signs that no longer refers to use-value, but to circulation. There is no consumption in a primal sense, or else it should be understood in an almost apocalyptic sense: the consumption of time, the using up of things.

SL: You didn't go to such extremes in *The Consumer Society* (1970), and yet you already realized that consumption was on its way to destroying the foundations of humanity. We've since made a good deal of progress in that direction.

JB: Yes, first one has to differentiate between consumption and consumation. Consumation is quite different; it doesn't involve signs anymore.

SL: You have been writing about consumption for more than thirty years. Is your analysis still valid today? Can we still say we are in a consumer society?

JB: To speak of consumption today sounds a bit anachronistic. In any case, the word consumption has been bandied about too much. And yet it doesn't mean that the form of this analysis has changed. Even if things haven't truly changed, one should speak about them differently. That is the problem I have been confronting since I returned to the question of "integral reality." I'm working to find another angle, something different. What I really like is taking the plunge: I write eight or ten pages and I am happy. Then I begin to wonder whether what I have written is so new after all. I go look at *Perfect Crime* or *The Transparency of Evil* and I realize it's already all there.

SL: You're simulating yourself?

JB: I'm cloning myself. [*Laughs*] It's not simulation; it's cloning. You retrace your own steps. Fortunately it's not quite linear. It's not accumulation. It always gets a little twisted.

SL: You have still demonstrated many times that the more things accumulate, the greater the chance for reversal. In *The Consumer Society* you said that one should expect that brutal irruptions or sudden negations as "unpredictable and unavoidable as May 1968 will come to shatter this white mass."

JB: I wrote that?

SL: Yes, you did. It's the conclusion to the book.

JB: Well, that's a good ending. [*Laughs*]

SL: But what does one do after the end? Now the question is whether the object will take its revenge on signs or whether information itself is consumed.

JB: Yes, it is consumed, of course. Because information is already beyond use-value, beyond reference. Consumption has already reached the information stage; it's no longer in the mirror stage – the mirror of production or consumption. We have gone through the screen. What is somewhat new is the dialectical balance between the two terms. One will always be able to connect consumption and information, for good reasons (and this doesn't mean the connection is false). Personally, I would make a distinction between them. I would say that something happened between consumption as a system of values, even as sign-value, and information, within information-technology: the murder, the disappearance of the sign. Not the murder of reality. I want to show that in information technology, in the virtual, digital system, there are no longer any signs in the first sense of referent, signifier, or signified. The sign's mediation, which establishes a kind of distance with the possibility of signifying if not reality, this mediation is impaired, raided by a type of binary digital language that is no longer a sign. We are no longer dealing with signs. That is the major change.

SL: The digital has replaced signs?

JB: Yes, the digital is not a sign, but a signal.

SL: Difference has taken refuge in the 0–1 interval?

JB: This isn't difference in the same sense that language makes differences. Language is a system of differences between signs. The interplay of signs in language through their differences is what allows for signification. In digital technology, this type of interplay is gone. It doesn't coordinate, it concatenates signals. It is information: you can move about it in any direction because there is no longer any mediation. There is an immanence, an immediation of things. That's what is new. It isn't the death of reality since reality as a whole passed into the sign. The sign absorbs reality. Images devour reality.

SL: And then images devour themselves.

JB: That is how we experience it. In consumption, there was an abstraction from use-value but there was a play of signs, signs of prestige as well as psychological and sociological signs … everything that was in Barthes' *Mythologies*. It was all there: the system of fashion, the system of objects. Then information technology reduced it all to the same level with an even greater abstraction where the sign disappears.

SL: It is not even simulation.

JB: It's beyond simulation.

SL: Sublimation in the strongest sense: transcendence.

JB: Yes. I see it as a kind of prolongation: passing from the object – the thing, the real – to the sign. In the next phase, which is beyond simulation, at the extreme reaches of simulation, one moves from the sign to something new: an immaterial form of the object, a kind of immense immaterial fetishism, which is the form of information. At the same time there is a shift from the mirror to the screen. The screen-phase is the reduction of signification, the end of the representation of signification. The screen is not a display-case, it's interactive. It's a transition. An interface is something other than a mirror. As long as we had the mirror of production, consumption, and signs, we had the possibility of going beyond it and then returning. But you cannot return from beyond the screen. It's immersion; it's definitive.

SL: In *The Consumer Society* you categorically challenged the legitimacy of any critical position, be it the Marxist discourse on alienation, the derision of Pop Art, or even anti-art. Counter-discourse was immanent to consumption. With information technology, even the illusion of distance becomes impossible.

JB: Consumption was the epitome of the critical stage. Sign-analysis was hypercritical, and often used. But critical consciousness faded in the consumer stage. The difficulty with the information stage is that it can no longer be made critical or reflexive. The only thing one can do is reject it or totally accept it, nothing else.

SL: If everything is critical, nothing is.

JB: Nothing is. It is a question of perspective. One can no longer find a critical distance. That is why I mentioned fetishism. In fetishism, sexuality becomes a pure object again. There is no distance, but rather total identification, total projection in the object. The fetish object is no longer a sign – it's an idol. So it can be a sock, a shoe, it doesn't matter. The fetish no longer signifies. There is no need to signify since you are stuck in it. You are immersed in it, combined with it. The signification, if there were one, would be sexual intercourse, but the sexual relation disappears; it is entirely realized in the fetish object.

SL: In *For a Critique of the Political Economy of the Sign*, you spoke of fetishism as a fascination that was not about making the object itself sacred, but a passion for code. You advanced the notion that the more systematic the system became, the more this fascination with code would grow. Now it is not even the sign-object that is emptied of substance, it is the sign-value. Abstract manipulation no longer bears a trace of difference; it is a pure difference that is no longer attached to anything, especially not itself. One can no longer speak of white or black magic, only of digital magic, an immaterial mirage. It is artifice as artifice.

JB: I must admit that in the face of this immersion in information technology, I feel like a foreigner, someone who barely partakes in it.

SL: You can see it better from the outside.

JB: You can see this immersion in the people who use it – they have no distance; they are completely absorbed by it. There is no possible reaction. I'll have to write something on the murder of the sign. I find it much more disturbing than the murder of reality.

SL: It isn't just that the digital leaves no traces, but that it never had any traces – the perfect crime.

JB: In that sense, yes. A perfect crime by obliteration. As long as there is substance and passion there is a crime: the death of God, or something like that. But this is *aphanisis*, the obliteration of things. You could already see it in consumption: when you pushed things farther, you ended up in circulation, in pure speculation. It was very close to the 0–1, except that here it is a series of 0–1 to infinity.

SL: It's like market speculation – I'm thinking of the Chicago Stock Exchange, not New York's. In Chicago, they speculate on money directly, not merchandise.

JB: On money, exactly. The ultimate stage of money is speculation, not exchange or specularization. There is nothing specular as in the reflective property of a mirror. We have information.

SL: You saw in the fascination with money the fetishizing of its virtuality. To speculate on money is to speculate on the virtuality of fetishization itself.

JB: With consumption, speculation was in its embryonic mode. We can now see that it consists in a whole logic that unfolds and goes to the extreme. At the same time, this doesn't prevent us from posing the genealogy of things. You can say that at a certain moment there is a rupture, a hiatus, a mutation. There is an irresistible revolution in abstraction and then a qualitative change. Information is its ultimate stage.

SL: Can we then analyze this mutation?

JB: You cannot analyze it. This mythology doesn't apply. You cannot find the image in the fragments. In his parable on the peoples of the mirror, Borges wrote: they are slaves to resemblance and representation; a day will come when they will try to stop resembling. They will go to the other side of the mirror and destroy the empire. But here, you cannot come back from the other side. The empire is on both sides.

SL: The strategy of consumption now tends to reverse itself. Some time ago already, Toffler declared that advertising had changed its meaning and that to some extent we no longer needed it. Rather than elicit the desire of consumers, their individual profile is established from various data banks and they are targeted with custom-tailored products. Consumers are no longer submitted to outside criteria; they become their own models.

JB: That's what happened in the "precession of the models," the ascendance of abstraction followed by a differential, but programmed lapse.

SL: Difference comes back at the end rather than being elicited at the outset.

JB: Yes, but is there still a subject of consumption?

SL: There is certainly a desire for difference.

JB: In the end, this desire is utopian. As for the need itself, it was critiqued in its time.

There is still a dimension of prestige in difference. In the computerized, technological, equipment-laden world, there are still prestige-effects, privilege-effects, but they are extremely reduced. The idea that one has the best computer does not last long. Yet it still holds, there is a kind of hope, to take up Pierre Bourdieu's theory. According to the logic of distinction, that he analyzed negatively, society does not function on equality but on a hierarchical system and the hereditary privilege of distinction. Bourdieu presented it as something to challenge through democracy. I say, on the contrary, that it is something precious that remains, an archaic remnant. It is still a human passion, something that saves us at least from a lack of differential distinction. It is better to have distinction even if there is some inequality and injustice. People still want to have the best computer, and you can see it in kids in the effect of performance. But I wonder if there is something that takes the upper hand on the information process itself, on the play of 0 and I; something that says: "It is not 0–I, it's me." I have asked this question: what remains of the logic of distinction in the logic of information? It seems, a priori, that information should annihilate distinction, but is that really a good thing?

SL: In fact, it has been recently revealed that companies fueled the rush for faster computers but people did not follow their lead as hoped. It seems they have reached a limit in the United States. Now the peripheral gadgets have taken the lead: miniature laptops that carry email, send photos, etc. People used to buy a computer every two years, but now they keep them longer. The computer itself is no longer an object of competition. This ceiling, this saturation is interesting. I don't know if it changes everything, but it means that something we counted on no longer works.

JB: Is it a limitation or a resistance? Is it that they have the feeling or fear of being manipulated?

SL: I'm not sure if the consumer has any awareness of this.

JB: Prestige and performance are two different sides. Do people say to themselves that this is enough performance, this is enough for them? No one needs a car that goes 300 miles per hour. In the logic of consumption, it should not stop, it should be inevitable and it is, fundamentally. There are still residual human elements. As machines are integrated, humans are forced to keep up with them. They make people excited, so when people hit the brakes, machines force them forward. They can't stop. There would have to be an ebb in the economy, and not just in the economy. There is a form of credibility in this acceleration. At the level of information technology, people are even more integrated. The consumer has become spontaneously interactive, because he or she is implicated like an accomplice in the unfolding of things. But here a corner has been turned, because consumers are their own managers in terms of knowledge.

SL: It's no longer exactly a consumer since this is no longer exactly a consumer society.

JB: This is a connection society. It is no longer possible to isolate an individual who is still responsible for a need or a passion. Everyone is interrelated now. People are passed through, they are no longer transitional objects. It's not even a question of passivity any more; everyone is both terminal and network. In the past, we blamed needs and passions. Now the focus is on a utopian functioning of the cerebral machine, everyone sensing each other in the cosmic cortex. The temptation is irresistible. They can play on it to infinity because we will soon have generations that have never known reality and will never have known signs either. They will be in the digit, in the digital. They won't even have any nostalgia for the sign. We are now in a period of transition.

SL: When Artaud sent his letters to Jacques Rivière, he was trying to see the real working of his cortex. He wanted to be sure that the words he uttered truly came from his brain and not from somewhere else. Some said Artaud was psychotic. But now society as a whole is like him.

JB: Yes, completely. That actually began with the brilliant English theoretician who deciphered all the German code systems during the war. He was condemned for homosexuality and ended up killing himself by eating an apple laced with poison. Of course, you think of Newton. Allegorically, this is a comic paradigm. Newton envisioned the invention of an astral and spectral body when the other bodily functions become useless.

SL: He probably developed that idea for trips to outer space.

JB: Yes, but he applied it according to the terms of the information technology sector. Everything hinges on that. He had the idea that we would reach the end of the biological, organic body and everything would be transposed into another body modeled on the brain. It was really McLuhan's total, extreme extension but completely restricted to the mind. All artificial intelligence comes from there.

SL: Is it a linear progression? We would go through a series of mutations and move towards an increasing level of abstraction?

JB: Yes, towards disappearance pure and simple.

SL: I often think of the Inca Empire that disappeared without leaving a trace. The volatilization, the murder of signs, is also a way of exterminating ourselves.

JB: Total reduction. A form of involution, if you like.

SL: That is what led DARPA to the Internet, the idea that there could be a nuclear explosion that would destroy everything immaterial. In fact, there's no longer a need for an atomic explosion.

JB: It would be a neutron bomb that left everything in place except humans.

SL: In the Catskills, they've dug an immense cave where they warehouse all electronic bank records. In the case of a nuclear explosion, they wanted to ensure that these accounts would be saved. It's a little dizzying. There would be no humans but there would still be a way to check accounts.

JB: That's not a bad story. You can imagine the face of those who find them, some Chinese people – there would still be a few – or extraterrestrials.

SL: The other day I was an hour late at the François Mitterrand National Library in Paris. The reservation for my seat had been electronically removed along with all the books I had requested. Everything has become so immaterial that nothing will be left of our civilization.

JB: It's a complete liquidation, an extermination, not even a death. There aren't any terms. It becomes integral reality. There is no strangeness, nothing that could be considered adversity, be it hostile or helpful, from an outside. One can only imagine a type of *alien* that would come to shatter all this.

SL: The alien is terrorism at present.

JB: Terrorism has emerged to make a kind of rupture, but it is only transitory.

SL: The true terrorism is ultimately that of the system itself.

REFERENCES

Barthes, Roland (1972), *Mythologies*. Trans. Annette Lavers. New York: Hill and Wang.

Baudrillard, Jean (1970), *The Consumer Society: Myths and Structures*. London, Thousand Oaks: Sage, 1998.

—— (1981), *For a Critique of the Political Economy of the Sign*. Trans. Charles Levin. St. Louis, Mo: Telos.

—— (1993), *Transparency of Evil: Essays on Extreme Phenomena*. Trans. James Benedict. London, New York: Verso.

—— (1996), *The Perfect Crime*. Trans. Chris Turner. London, New York: Verso.

Part I

Cultural Consumption in an Age of Information

CHAPTER 2

Future Advertising: Dick's Ubik and the Digital Ad

Mark Poster

Consumption changes significantly in the age of digital information. Acts of consumption – buying, window-shopping, browsing – are routinely recorded, stored and made available for advertisers. Profiles of the lifestyles of consumers are now so finely granulated and accurate that retailers are likely to know better than the consumer what he or she will buy and when the purchase will take place. Automated programs on one's computer, known as "bots," have better memories of consumer preferences than does the consumer. Information machines such as TiVo gather data of viewing habits and on that basis anticipate consumer desires for entertainment. The individual finds himself/herself in a brave new world of consumption, prefigured only in the imagination of science fiction writers. I shall investigate the current condition of consumption by reading closely one such work of science fiction, Philip K. Dick's *Ubik*, a work that presciently depicts the future of advertising.

It can be argued that the genre of science fiction is no longer possible. This is so for the simple reason that what some call the overdeveloped nations have so integrated into their social processes scientific achievements, technological novelties, and, above all, the system for the continued, indefinite development of science and technology that the distance has collapsed between what can be imagined in science fiction and what has been realized or can be foreseen to be realized in society. Science fiction requires the sense of a future as separate from the present. But this future is now part of the present expectations of everyday life. We anticipate that nanotechnology will make obsolete industrial labor; that cloning of human beings will initiate ethical dilemmas; that worldwide communication systems will bring about the demise of the nation state. These expectations are the life-world of the present and as such cannot be regarded as a future "other." With the proliferation of cyborgs, robots, clones, and androids, the age of the humachine has arrived. The future tense will have to be reimagined, probably outside the genre of science fiction. The social imaginary has integrated the research agendas of science and technology to such an extent that the future is imploded into the present. In a sense, there can be no more aliens.

In this spirit I shall explore the relation between Philip K. Dick's *Ubik* and the mediascape that we call the hyperreal. In particular, I shall examine the culture of advertising by comparing the representation of commodities in print and digital media. More specifically I shall compare, in the context of *Ubik,* the cultural role of the representation of commodities in print with that in various forms of digital ads. At issue is the difference of print and visual forms, analogue and digital formats. As a genre, science fiction has the advantage of exploring the relation of humans to machines,[1] a relation that has become a general aspect of the human condition. For quite some time, science fiction has been exploring what we now accept as the post-human. With the multiplication and dissemination of increasingly advanced information machines, the Earth has entered a post-human era. Our society has done so under the general regime of the commodity, which, at the cultural level, disseminates itself in the discourse of advertising.[2] Dick's novel explores the *Ubik*quity of the ad and its relation to the formation of a humanity that is synthesized with information machines. In this essay I shall examine Dick's representation of the culture of the ad, with an eye to the light it sheds on the current state of advertising in new media. I shall ask if the digital form of the ad changes anything with respect to the construction of the subject? Does it matter that cyberspace is filled with ads, that ads on television are more and more produced with computer technology? Are we heading toward the world of Dick's *Ubik*?

In a strange confluence of events, Philip K. Dick's *Ubik* was published in 1969,[3] the year of the first transmissions of information across telephone lines between computers, a technology now known as the Internet. Stranger still perhaps, Dick's novel is set in June 1992, some eight months before

Mosaic, the first web browser, was distributed on the Internet, signaling a transformation of the Net into graphic format and foreshadowing its mass adoption. In these coincidences, print media and digital media, separated by centuries of technical development, met, crossed, and went their separate ways.

My reading of *Ubik* has a limited purpose. I am not attempting to provide a decisive interpretation of the novel as a whole, but to examine one aspect of it. In the space provided, I cannot situate it systematically in relation to Dick's other works,[4] science fiction writing of the period, nor in general, although I shall discuss some of Dick's other work and the work of some scholars in relation to certain questions. I shall focus neither on the author's relation to the text nor on reviewing the corpus of scholarly treatment of the text. The specific theme I wish to consider is the way the novel depicts a world in which culture is shaped by mediated information. In this sense, Dick's portrayal of such a world may assist us in understanding more about our own circumstances. The question of the media is central to this culture of information. I shall examine the issue of media in the work at three levels: the printed form of the novel itself, the role of mediated information in the imaginary world of *Ubik*, and the relation of this world to the digital culture of the present.

UBIK'S *STORY*

For readers familiar with Dick's work and with science fiction writing in general, the plot of *Ubik* will not come as a big surprise, but to those not conversant with the conventions of the genre, a plot summary of *Ubik* might appear as preposterous as that of most nineteenth-century operas. With this warning to the reader, I proceed with my summary.

Set in the near future, *Ubik* opens with a crisis in a security company, Runciter Associates, which is having difficulty tracking individuals whose extraordinary psychic powers make them dangerous information thieves. The band of these "psis" is headed by Ray Hollis, an antagonist who never appears in the novel. Glen Runciter, president of the company, and his chief tester for psionic fields, Joe Chip, attempt to account for the strange, sudden invisibility of the telepathic individuals. In *Ubik*'s world information is central and it is made fragile by "teeps, parakineticists, precogs, resurrectors and animators" (Dick, 1969: 17) – an assortment of abilities to act at a distance through brain power, abilities which today, we might note, are simulated by a variety of information technologies. Runciter Associates is solicited by companies to counter the effects of the telepaths. It employs "inertials," individuals who, for example, make it impossible for those who see the future to decide which future is most likely to occur. In these unusual encounters, to understate the matter, *Ubik* anticipates the collapse of privacy that today is achieved through machines. No one is safe from the prying minds of the psis. There is no interior space that provides a safe haven for information, desire, anything one might rather not make available to others.

In addition to telepaths, society is composed of another group who act through brain power alone, the half-lifers. These are individuals who have, in our sense of the term, died but whose brain is kept in a minimal state of activity, enough so that they are able to communicate, in a manner of speaking, with living humans. Again the novel presents a group whose bodies, like the psis', have little importance. Like Hans Moravec (1988), who would have us cast off our meat and upload our consciousness to the Internet, Dick explores states of being which minimize the importance of the body. Glen Runciter's wife, Ella, exists in such a state in what Dick calls a "Moratorium" in, of all places, Switzerland.

The action continues when Runciter is approached by a woman who wants to hire his firm to counter an alleged breach of security in a company located on the Moon. Runciter believes the psis that are missing from his intelligence maps are engaged in this information attack. He takes his inertials to the Moon. But the job is actually a trap set by archenemy Hollis and Runciter's people are killed, or more accurately reduced to cryogenic half-life.

From the social world of information security issues, the novel at this point shifts focus to the world of the half-lifers and to the communication between them and those who are alive in the normal sense of the word. It must be emphasized here that Dick makes undecidable who is in half-life and who is not. We will return to this issue later. Among the nominally half-life individuals is a teenage boy, Jory, who sustains himself by "eating" the brain activity of the others in the Moratorium, the storage facility for half-lifers. Earlier, when Glen Runciter visited his wife, his communications with her were blocked by Jory, who displaced her weak brain activity with his own. Jory's prey have only one defense against him, a "product" known as Ubik, a "reality support" that protects the half-lifers by emitting substances into the atmosphere that interfere with Jory's predations. Since the half-lifers sustain only mental activity, I find it difficult to understand how the reader is expected to accept that a material effect from Ubik can intervene in their communications. Such are the imponderables of the genre, however.

The last third of the novel concerns the efforts of the half-lifers, Joe Chip in particular, to defend themselves against Jory. They are assisted by Glen Runciter who manages to communicate to the half-lifers across reality systems about the great powers of Ubik.

There is another subplot that is essential to understanding the book. As in many Dick stories, *Ubik* includes a beautiful young woman, a "dark-haired girl," who attracts the protagonist, in this case Joe Chip, and appears to threaten him at the same time. In *Ubik* this character is Pat Conley, a person who has the extrasensory ability to move time backwards and thereby change the future. After the attack on Runciter's employees on the Moon the world appears to be in a state of regression. The inertials appear at once to age very quickly, suggesting that time is flowing rapidly into the future, and to experience external reality as moving into the past, suggesting a process of entropy so dear to Dick's understanding of physical reality. The reader and some of the characters think that Pat Conley is responsible for these disastrous happenings but that turns out not to be the case. Jory is the villain. The ageing and regression are effects of the condition of half-life. They do not affect external reality. They are only the perception of the half-life population as they undergo death at the hands of Jory.

Ubik is, even for science fiction, a strange work, combining the exotica of science fiction such as telepaths and half-lifers with the mundane objects of commodity culture. I suggest that it offers a picture of the hyperreal world of mediated information through the rhetorical techniques of science fiction.

MEDIA IN UBIK

Dick is sensitive to changes in media, to new media, to the role of media in people's lives. For example, in a passage of no particular importance to the plot he takes the trouble to forecast an electronic newspaper (a "homeopape") much like what currently exists on the Internet. One can format the homeopape to deliver one's personally designed newspaper. Here is Dick's description of the media: "Joe Chip ... twiddled the dial of his recently rented 'pape machine ... he dialed off *interplan news*, hovered momentarily at *domestic news* and then selected *gossip*." In Dick's world, the 'pape can speak: "'Yes sir,' the 'pape machine said heartily." And it is able to print out one's selections in color and chosen fonts: "... a scroll of printed matter crept from its slot; the ejected roll, a document in four colors, niftily incised with bold type." It also has the capability of voice recognition: "'This isn't gossip,' Joe Chip said to the 'pape machine." In response to the character's dissatisfaction with the news delivered to him, the machine gives instructions regarding its proper use. "The 'pape machine said, 'Set the dial for *low gossip*.'" Like today's intelligent agent programs and help menus, the Dick's machine provides users with feedback on its best use. (Dick, 1969: 19–20) Although Dick does not explain how the machine obtains newspaper information, the reader must assume some electronic connection between the machine and a database of current news, in principle much like the Internet's ability to store and to distribute information to any computer.

Ubik is not different in respect from much of Dick's other work in its sensitivity and prescience about information machines. In one novel, *The Penultimate Truth*, the spiritual leader of the nation is literally constructed by media, the person having died years before. Protector Talbot Yancy, his image broadcast on "giant television screens," urges the Western Democracies on to battle in their interminable and disastrous war with the Soviet Union. Humans live underground because of radiation, in a miserable, bellicose existence. Set in the early part of the twenty-first century, this novel, published in 1964, explores with remarkable attention to detail the simulation effects possible with information machines. In the following passage a character observes the simulation of Yancy with awe:

"I take off my hat to you. You're good." He had almost been captured himself, as he had stood watching the simulacrum of the Protector Talbot Yancy deliver the absolutely the proper intonation, the exact and correct manner, the text modified and augmented – meddled with – by Magavac 6-V and although this was not visible could sense the emanation of the reading matter directed by the 'vac toward the simulacrum. Could in fact witness the true source which animated the purely artificial construct seated at the oak desk with the American flag behind it. Eerie, he thought. (Dick, 1984: 59)

The Penultimate Truth sets out with precision the emergence and logical conclusion of televisual politics. In Dick's hands, information media transform political reality into a web of images and sounds that are impossible to refer back to a referent. Politics, for him, have already, by dint of the media, transcended agora-like community and representational logics, moving into the constructed effects perhaps best realized in the Gulf War of 1991.[5] We can recall that, thanks to such media, Jean Baudrillard quipped that "the war did not take place" (Baudrillard, 1995). Dick understood that media change reality, an insight that became central to New Left politics a few years after the publication of *The Penultimate Truth*. As the United States entered the colonial conflict with Vietnam in 1964, leading to the televisual politics of phony consensus by Lyndon Johnson and to the televised films of combat that catalyzed anti-war sentiment, Dick presented cold-war political leadership as bound with mediated propaganda images.

In another novel from the same period as *The Penultimate Truth* and *Ubik*, *The Ganymede Takeover*, Dick manifests a sharp recognition of the importance of advertisements, especially those disseminated on television. He writes concerning the views of one of his characters: "How much he had learned from TV commercials! While others turned down the TV set when the commercials came on, Balkani turned them up. The programs had nothing to sell but middle-class morality, a dreary product at best, but the commercial offered a world where dreams were for sale, where youth and health came in a box, and all pain and suffering were smoothed over with long, beautiful, slow-motion hair. Avant-garde films? Balkani jeered at them. Nothing lay in the most surrealistic of them to compare with the charisma of TV commercials" (Dick & Nelson, 1967: 132). The culture of advertising and media become central to Dick's sense of the construction of reality. The mediated world of commodities plays a pivotal role for Dick in the functioning of fictional worlds. TV ads are not trivial, obnoxious interference with entertainment; nor are they artless products of pecuniary impulses. They are instead the spiritual center of the world, far more worthy of visual attention, Dick mocks at pretentious high culture, than experimental cinema.

The media then, for Dick, are significant in their ability to alter culture (and politics), to work miracles on symbolic systems. Let us consider then this mixture of commercialism and media within the limits of print.

THE PRINT MEDIA

The novel consists of seventeen chapters, each starting with an epigraph. The first sixteen epigraphs are advertisements for a product called "Ubik." Here is the epigraph to the first chapter: "Friends, this is clean-up time and we're discounting all our silent, electric Ubiks by this much money. Yes, we're throwing away the blue-book. And remember: every Ubik on our lot has been used only as directed" (Dick, 1969: 1). Each advertisement is for a different product. They are cars, beer, coffee, salad dressing, headache and stomach medicine, shaving razor, kitchen cleaning aid, a bank, hair conditioner, deodorant spray, sleeping pills, breakfast food, bra, plastic wrap, breath freshener, and cereal, a list of ordinary consumer objects. Each ad contains a warning to the consumer like "Safe when used as directed." None of the ads have any direct relation to the chapter they introduce. The chapter preceded by the ad for beer, for instance, contains no mention of beer or any beverage for that matter. Rather the ads appear on the printed page like commercials on radio and television, interrupting the flow of the program, distracting the reader/viewer's attention from what has come before and what will follow, yet also justifying the text/program, as we shall see. Dick uses the epigraph, a device of the print medium, to emulate electronic broadcast media. In fact the tone of the epigraphs resembles the audio portion of ads in electronic media. The epigraphic voice is informal, plain, and solicitous, more like television than other print media such as magazines and newspapers. Dick's chapter epigraphs work against the limits and constraints of the conventional print format in which they serve as emblems or metonymies for the text that ensues, distinguishing themselves by their complete irrelevance to the body of the chapter.

In their discontinuity with the chapters, the ads however do inject commodity culture (in its print-mediated form) into the work. They provide a mood of commercialism, a spirit of the commodity that operates outside the story (for the most part) but nonetheless informs a general cultural character to the work. The ads address the reader as a member of a mediated (capitalist) culture. Further in that direction are the frequent small reminders of a money economy: for example, in apartments, doors and small appliances (such as coffee makers) require coins to operate. Dick leaves nothing to the reader's imagination concerning the capitalist nature of the world of *Ubik*. Yet this capitalism has a decidedly informational quality. Runciter Associates, once again, is a security firm that provides antidotes to information piracy. True enough, the thieves are not mechanical but psionic, individuals with extraordinary psychic abilities. The effect however is very much the same as the security problems in late capitalism or postmodern society where information machines penetrate protected physical space to retrieve private data. The "psis," as Dick calls them, substitute easily for computerized databases hooked into networks, listening devices, global positioning systems, satellite photography, and the rest, culminating in a society where nothing can be hidden or secret.

The epigraphs then are an integral part of a general set up in which information is central to the social system, whether as advertising or as security issues. Although not the first writer to discover this insight, Dick senses that culture is becoming political and becoming mediated. It is also becoming vulnerable and at risk.

About two-thirds of the way through the novel, the term Ubik enters the story directly, leaving the confines of the epigraph to intrude upon the text of the chapter. Ubik appears first in the text as a televised commercial, providing a link with the epigraphs. "Has boiled cabbage taken over your world of food? That same old, stale, flat, Monday-morning odor no matter how many dimes you put into your stove? Ubik changes all that; Ubik wakes up food flavor, puts hearty taste back where it belongs, and restores fine food smell," announces Glen Runciter on his employee, Joe Chip's television

(Dick, 1969: 127). At this point, Joe thinks Runciter is either dead or in a half-life coma. The reader learns later that the reverse is true, or apparently true since, in Dick's novels, reality is always in question for the characters and the reader.[6] The commercial goes on to speak of what emerges as Ubik's true function, a "reality support." The world around the half-life of Joe Chip is regressing temporally and Ubik is Runciter's proposed solution for the problem. In a wider sense, Ubik is the elixir for life's difficulties; commodities offer, as we recall from *The Ganymede Takeover*, a spiritual antidote to life's misery, the dream of gratification. When Runciter on the TV ad urges Joe to try Ubik, we are all addressed as users of commodities.

At first the role of Ubik is a mystery to the characters, just as it is to consumers in capitalist society. Gradually its wondrous powers become clear to the protagonists, Joe Chip and the other employees of Runciter Associates. It seems they have died physically and are being sustained in a sort of cryogenic hospital surviving only in their brain function. They are assailed by Jory and can protect themselves from his predations with the use of Ubik. Thus Ubik, the reality support, functions as an information shield or spiritual shell that maintains the brain activity of half-life. Or at least that is what the narrative suggests at a literal level. From our perspective in understanding *Ubik* as an allegory of mediated culture, we can say that commodities such as Ubik sustain consumers in their reality as a kind of half-life in capitalist culture. If Joe Chip and the others are metaphors for consumers in information capitalism, then Ubik (a synecdoche for all commodities) sustains cultural life against dangers of all kinds (represented by Jory).

In addition to its epigraphic role as ubiquitous commodity and as reality support in consumer culture, Ubik has a third role in the novel, one that is most difficult to interpret. The last chapter's epigraph reads as follows: "I am Ubik. Before the universe was, I am. I made the suns. I made the worlds. I created the lives and the places they inhabit; I move them here, I put them there. They go as I say, they do as I tell them. I am the word and my name is never spoken, the name which no one knows. I am called Ubik, but that is not my name. I am. I shall always be" (Dick, 1969: 215). The ad for Ubik now sounds much like the voice of God in the opening of *Genesis*.[7] Interpreting this epigraph has been a focus of scholarly attention and to that I shall now turn.

GOD UBIK?

Katherine Hayles summarizes the discussion of the final epigraph[8] and offers her own interpretation of the strange epigraph. Hayles muses,

> To my knowledge, no one has attempted to explain why Ubik changes from signifying the worst excesses of capitalism to standing for a ubiquitous God. Many critics even suggest that Ubik has somehow "really" been God all along. I want to suggest that on the contrary, Ubik undergoes a sudden transformation and that this transformation cannot be understood except in relation to the revelation that behind Pat stands Jory and behind Jory stands his animalistic appetite. Only after acknowledging this appetite (which must be understood as operating on the multiple levels signified by "consuming") can the author discern, among the trashy surfaces of capitalist excess, the divine within the world – and by implication, within himself. (Hayles, 1999: 187)

In short, Hayles explains the contrast between the epigraphs of the first sixteen chapters with that of the last chapter as a Gnostic revelation of God within the beast of capitalist culture. But this leads her to a more general argument concerning language itself. For Hayles, Dick's novel explores and deconstructs the boundary of the human individual and the world, the line between the inside and the outside. Language in the form of media draws into permanent instability the ontological demarcation of the human. Hayles concludes her argument,

> *Ubik's* distinctive achievement is to represent *simultaneously* the performative power of language and the mediated, uncertain relation of language to the material world while also mapping this difference onto an "inside"–"outside" boundary that hints at the complexity of communication between self and other, conscious and unconscious. The hope *Ubik* holds out is that although boundary disputes will never disappear, inside and outside can be made to touch each other through the medium of writing that is no less valuable for infecting our world with all manner of epistemological and ontological instabilities. (Hayles, 1999: 188)

For Hayles, the issue at stake in the final epigraph is neither God nor capitalism but the relation of writing to the self. Her interest in the novel, certainly an important interpretative stance, rests with literature and culture.

I offer a somewhat different interpretation of the last epigraph and of the novel as a whole. It is necessary to consider the *combination* of the ordinary commercials in the first sixteen epigraphs, the seemingly religious last epigraph, the role of Ubik in the action of the novel as reality support, and the literal meaning of the word ubiquitous as existing everywhere, a meaning that is discussed by the characters in the novel. If we take these four instances of Ubik together we are confronted with a culture permeated by commercials such that reality is sustained by them. People are steeped in the culture of advertising. They are able to maintain their sense of reality only by imbibing commodity culture. They resist life's threats, such as Jory, by heeding commercials. If the half-lifers are understood to represent the general population of consumer culture, living in the hyperreal world of mediated information, their identities then persist through that culture. Incursions by individuals with strong emotions, like Jory, endanger the continuity of the consumerist world. Even if we accept this argument, the dilemma of the last epigraph is not resolved. To do that, we must find a connection between religion, the ultimate spiritual force, and commodities.

Such a connection was explored by Walter Benjamin in his Arcades Project (Benjamin, 1999). Fascinated by the panorama of objects of capitalist society and the aesthetics of their presentation, Benjamin extended Marx's analysis of the fetishism of commodities. For Marx, a commodity became invested with more interest than it intrinsically had (hence became a fetish), because the labor that produced was secreted from its appearance on the market. The outrage for Marx and the force of his critique focused on the disappearance of the labor act from the activity of consumption. Benjamin looked beyond that perception to the phantasmagoria of the commodities themselves. "With the new manufacturing processes that leads to imitations," he wrote, "an illusory appearance (*Schein*) settles into the commodity" (Buck-Morss, 1991: 191). The work of critique for Benjamin subsisted at the level of the appearance of the commodity, supplementing Marx's depth analysis of the commodity in relation to the production process. Benjamin's "dialectics of seeing," as Susan Buck-Morss has termed the method of the Arcades Project, revealed, among its other insights into daily life, the relation of the appearance of the commodity on the capitalist market to religious experience. Walking through the streets of Paris, Benjamin's highly original ethnography of consumerism introduced the eye of the *flâneur*, one whose consciousness retreated from the heights of focused philosophical acumen and systematic self-reflection (let us call it Kantian consciousness), and, with body in motion, loosely regarded the things in the urban environment with the curiosity of a child.[9] In the state of mind of the *flâneur*, commodities appeared as magical, as invested with spiritual properties of myth, aura, and sublimity. Here was a new sublime of the everyday, one that transported the would-be consumer to a transcendent world of fulfillment, a heavenly redemption from the arduous exigencies of capitalism. The most exquisite supernatural qualities were found not in the cathedrals but in the objects before one's gaze in store windows.

Dick noted the same link of commodity culture with high spiritual values in the passage quoted above from *The Ganymede Takeover*, except here the everyday sublime pertained not to the commodity itself but the solicitation to it, the advertisement. Dick recognized more directly than Benjamin that the spirit of capitalism rests not with the commodity as object, but with the culture developed to promote it, with, as he says in the seventeenth epigraph, the word. What enables the seventeenth epigraph to work as a link to the earlier ones and to the play of Ubik in the novel is that commercials are cultural objects, strings of words, images, and sounds. And they are so arranged as to fascinate all who encounter them. They constitute the highest promise of happiness and fulfillment of any experience in capitalist society. Dick's novel recognizes the spiritual force of the commercial.[10] When Dick paraphrases the Old Testament with "I am Ubik.... I am the word ... I am..." (1969: 215), he perhaps at one level introduces the voice of God but at another, and in my view far more significant, level he invokes the highest spiritual force, the force that is the ultimate "reality support," as the cultural dimension of the capitalist solicitation, of the ad.

DIGITAL DICK?

If the reader is with me so far, I would like to take one step further in the analysis: to account for the fact that, since at least the second half of the twentieth century, commercials appear primarily in mediated form, specifically transmitted through the airways and wires of the electronic media. As we have seen in relation to the 'pape in *Ubik* and the computer simulation in *The Penultimate Truth*, Dick was highly aware of the effectiveness of media and was aware of their specific traits. Visual media achieve certain effects, print others and audio still others. How then was Dick to present the qualities of electronic media through the limitations of print media? How could Dick suggest the culture of televised commercials with the specific attributes of the printed page? It is this problem, I believe, that he attempted to solve by use of the seventeenth epigraph.

Friedrich Kittler reminds us of the limits of print as a storage medium. Without the ability to store sounds and moving images, the printed page cannot achieve the spectacular effects of cinema, television, the World Wide Web. He advises,

> Writing can store only writing, no more, no less. The holy books testify to this fact. The second book of Moses, chapter twenty, fixes a copy of what Jaweh originally had written with his own finger on two stone tablets: the law. Of the thunder and lightning, the dense cloud and very powerful trumpet that accompanied the writing-down on the holy mountain of Sinai, The Bible could store nothing but mere words. (Kittler & Johnston, 1997: 37)

And Dick in *Ubik* could not store and transmit to the reader the magic of the commercial except by referring back to that volume. Kittler argues that, due to the limitations of the printed page, words are obliged to stimulate in the reader a "hallucination" of the scene, a poetic imaginary that produces in the mind the very absences apparent in the page: the sounds of thunder and trumpets, the clouds and the lightning, etc. Dick, with his seventeenth epigraph, summons that imaginary with an allusion to the Bible.

If the mediascape of the 1960s, when *Ubik* was written, was dominated by cinema and television, we have moved on, since the mid-1990s, to the digital transformation of cultural objects – text, sounds and images – and to their global storage and transmission on the World Wide Web. And if televised commercials were the "reality support," the Ubik, of the 1960s (and the early 1990s when *Ubik* is set), so digital technology now increasingly dominates the task of encouraging consumers to buy the effluence of late capitalism. The message of *Ubik* is a warning about the ontological capacities of the analogue advertisement, its seemingly limitless ability to create reality. If that is so, what might be the nature of the reality support of the post-analogue world of digital culture?

Dick's insight into the spiritual qualities of contemporary media culture deploys the genre of science fiction to express itself. We might ask if this same genre is capable of translating for us the media effects of digital culture? To some degree Dick anticipated this development. He certainly included computers in his novels. But more than that, he depicted phenomena that could only be realized with the development of digital culture. I refer to his anticipation of virtual reality systems (the helmet and glove variety, or the cave) in the short story "We Can Remember It For You Wholesale" (1966), in which a company is able to provide customers with experiences by implanting information in their brains. Many such novelties are strewn through the pages of Dick's novels and short stories. The question remains if the genre can sustain its own realization, so to speak, if the digital culture of the Internet has not brought forth a mediated construction of reality that the features of science fiction now inhabit the earth.

One direction that the genre of science fiction has taken in response to digital culture is cyberpunk. Starting with William Gibson's 1984 novel, *Neuromancer*, a spate of work by Gibson, Bruce Sterling, Pat Cadigan, Neal Stephenson, and others has explored the theme of digital culture in future worlds. Writers have addresses many aspects of networked computing, among them the struggle for information security. This is the leitmotiv of Neal Stephenson's recent novel, *Cryptonomicon* (1999). Stephenson's fascinating work (Stephenson) juxtaposes the work of decoding communications during World War II with a contemporary project to build a "data haven" in a location somewhere near the Philippines. The double temporality of the work highlights the historical importance of the question of information security. And indeed the potential of the privacy of records and other information in the circuits of the Internet threatens the security of the nation state. In the 1940s, information access was crucial in determining the outcome of the contest between Germany/Japan and the United States/Britain/the Soviet Union, all nation states. But by 2000, the nation state itself was in jeopardy, or at least saw itself as in jeopardy, as a consequence of the digital network.[11] *Cryptonomicon*'s fictional representation of a possible data haven suggests that information security is the dream of a host of unsavory types: drug dealers, mafia groups, terrorists, gamblers, dealers in illegal commodities from weapons to body parts, slave traders – you name it. But data privacy is also the desire of countless others. Since the nation state is the dominant political force, one that claims right of access to all information within its territory, it is the default enemy of the data haven. Stephenson's novel unfortunately gets sidetracked from exploring the ramifications of the data haven, turning instead to a hunt for gold bullion lost in World War II, and thus ironically mirroring those entrepreneurs from the mid to late 1990s who treated the Internet not as an experiment in communications but as a gold rush.

In conclusion, I suggest for future exploration that the question of information privacy dovetails nicely with Dick's exploration of the mediated commercial in *Ubik*, indicating that capitalism's effort to commodify culture runs into difficulty at several levels in the digital domain. A new contradiction of capitalism emerges in digital culture whereby the urge to sell commodities comes into conflict with the need for private information. Since all commercial transactions are digitally recorded and stored in databases, information about acts of consumption are compiled to such an extent that portraits of consumers are available for general commercial exploitation, in other words, for targeted advertising.[1] In the digital age, shopping is no longer private, even when it is done inside one's home. Capitalism, it appears, cannot have its cake of a zone of commodified culture and eat it as well, so to speak, in the private. The future of digital advertising will be ubiquitous at the cost of a kind of blowback effect in which corporate databases are open to hackers/consumers. If the world, as in *Ubik*, is made available for the dissemination of commercials, the sources of that dissemination will be open as well to public scrutiny.

NOTES

1. For an exploration of this argument see (Mirzoeff, 1999: Chapter 6). Also helpful for a general approach to the genre of science fiction film is Sobchack (1997).

2. Many scholars and theorists have explored the relation of media to consumer culture. The History of this relation is well developed in Marchand (1985). Also noteworthy are Featherstone (1991) and Firat and Dholakia (1998). On the relation of advertising to the latest developments in consumer technology, see the informative newspaper article Harmon (2002).

3. For bibliographic information on Philip K. Dick, see Levack (1988).

4. See, for example, Pohl and Kornbluth (1953).

5. Dick had already explored the theme of the virtual political leader in *The Simulacra* (1964).

6. At first the reader feels confident that Glen Runciter escaped the bomb explosion on the Moon and is alive whereas Joe Chip and the other employees are in a half-life state. But on the last page of the novel Runciter gives someone coins that have the profile of Joe Chip on them and the narrator warns Runciter in the final works of the novel: "This was just the beginning" (216). Earlier, Joe Chip had received funny money with Runciter's image imprinted and this was part of many events that, the reader thought, were Runciter's efforts to communicate to the half-life people. But now, the reverse appears to be the case: that Runciter is in the half-life and Joe Chip is trying to communicate with him. This ambiguous reality is common to Dick's work and underlines the fact that there is no stable grasp on reality among any of the characters in the novel, hence, no stable grasp on reality as objective anywhere.

7. Although it is from The Gospel of John 8:58: "Jesus said unto them [the Jews]. Verily, verily, I say unto you, Before Abraham was, I am."

8. Carl Freedman, for example, interprets the last epigraph in relation to the theme of paranoia in Dick's novels. (Freedman, 1995) Peter Fitting (1976) presents a Marxist view of the novel as a whole and the epigraph in particular. Both essays were published first in *Science Fiction Studies*, the leading journal in the field. Carl Freedman also devoted a chapter to Dick in *Critical Theory and Science Fiction* (2000), although it does not treat *Ubik*.

9. See also the important work of Anne Friedberg (1993), who suggestively terms this state of consciousness a mobile virtual gaze.

10. I am not interested in Dick's personal views of religion but rather in the way the "religious" epigraph works in the text in question.
11. For an excellent discussion of the effort by the Clinton administration to defeat privacy on the Internet through encryption systems, see Gurak (1997).
12. See Tedeschi (2003) for a report on the use of "interactive ads" in which companies sell information about online browsing to other companies.

REFERENCES

Baudrillard, Jean (1995), *The Gulf War Did Not Take Place*. Bloomington: Indiana University Press.

Benjamin, Walter (1999), *The Arcades Project*. Trans. Howard Eiland and Kevin McLaughlin. Cambridge: Belknap Press.

Buck-Morss, Susan (1991), *The Dialectics of Seeing: Walter Benjamin and the Arcades Project*. Cambridge: MIT Press.

Dick, Philip K. (1964), *The Simulacra*. New York: Ace.

—— (1969) *Ubik*. New York: Vintage.

—— (1984), *The Penultimate Truth*. New York: Carroll & Graf.

—— and Ray Nelson (1967), *The Ganymede Takeover*. London: Legend.

Featherstone, Mike (1991), *Consumer Culture and Postmodernism*. London: Sage.

Firat, Fuat and Nikhilesh Dholakia (1998), *Consuming People: From Political Economy to Theaters of Consumption*. New York: Routledge.

Fitting, Peter (1976), "Ubik: The Deconstruction of Bourgeois SF," in R. D. Mullen and Darko Suvin (eds), *Science-Fiction Studies: Selected Articles on Science Fiction, 1973–1975*. Boston: Gregg Press, pp. 203–9.

Freedman, Carl (2000), *Critical Theory and Science Fiction*. Hanover, N.H.: Wesleyan University Press.

Freedman, Carl (1995), "Towards a Theory of Paranoia: The Science Fiction of Philip K. Dick," in Samuel Umland (ed.), *Philip K. Dick: Contemporary Critical Interpretations*. Westport, Conn.: Greenwood Press, pp. 7–17.

Friedberg, Anne (1993), *Window Shopping: Cinema and the Postmodern*. Berkeley: University of California Press.

Gibson, William (1984), *Neuromancer*. New York: Ace Books.

Gurak, Laura (1997), *Persuasion and Privacy in Cyberspace: The Online Protests over Lotus Marketplace and the Clipper Chip*. New Haven: Yale University Press.

Harmon, Amy (2002), "Digital Video Recorders Give Advertisers Pause." *New York Times*, May 23.

Hayles, N. Katherine (1999), *How We Became Posthuman: Virtual Bodies in Cybernetics, Literature, and Informatics*. Chicago: University of Chicago Press.

Kittler, Friedrich A. and John Johnston (1997), *Essays: Literature, Media, Information Systems*. Critical Voices in Art, Theory and Culture. Amsterdam: G+B Arts International.

Levack, Daniel (1988), *PKD: A Philip K. Dick Bibliography*. London: Meckler Corporation.

Marchand, Roland (1985), *Advertising and the American Dream: Making Way for Modernity, 1920–1940*. Berkeley: University of California Press.

Mirzoeff, Nicholas (1999), *An Introduction to Visual Culture*. New York: Routledge.

Moravec, Hans (1988), *Mind Children: The Future of Robot and Human Intelligence*. Cambridge: Harvard University Press.

Pohl, Frederik and Cyril Kornbluth (1953), *The Space Merchants*. New York: Ballantine Books.

Sobchack, Vivian (1997), *Screening Space: The American Science Fiction Film*, 2nd edition. New Brunswick, NJ: Rutgers University Press.

Stephenson, Neal (1999), *Cryptonomicon*. New York: Harper Collins.

Tedeschi, Bob (2003), "E-Commerce Report: If You Liked the Web Page, You'll Love the Ad," Web page. *New York Times*, Aug 4. Available: http://www.nytimes.com/2003/08/04/technology/04ECOM.html.

CHAPTER 3

Spending Time

Tom Lutz

Time is the coin of your life. It is the only coin you have, and only you can determine how it will be spent. Be careful lest you let other people spend it for you.

Carl Sandburg

Time is relative, we can all agree. But what does this mean exactly? I think being ten minutes late for lunch is fine; others are insulted. Are they just being touchy, or, as I have been told, is that simply a narcissistic bit of after-the-fact rationalizing on my part? In either case, the ten minutes feel different to the person waiting than they do to the person who is late: two different experiences, two different durations, in Jamesian or Bergsonian terms. This is an obviously trivial example, but what about the larger questions of relative time? Are "traditional society" and "modernity" simply qualitative, durational differences, as Johannes Fabian (1983) for one has argued, rather than, as suggested by the very ideas of "modernization" or "development," moments in a historical progression? Should we be thinking about the divisions in our world in terms of time? Isn't "development" itself a polluted term, a betrayal of its user's teleological faith? We might agree with Fabian that anthropologists are in error when they deny the contemporaneity of the cultures they study, without agreeing that our own industrial time, the "time of the commodity," as John Frow (1997) calls it, is simply one kind of time among many, with no special status despite its obvious hegemony, except in some trivially theoretical sense. All times may be equal, but the power they exercise is clearly not. The clock rules. And, still, there is enough relativity left to put serious strains on our everyday relationships, on our very lunches.

People who want to insist on the relativity of time love to cite the Einsteinian example of a man who flies through space at close to the speed of light while his twin brother stays on earth. The flier comes back younger than the earthbound brother because of what is known as the Lorentz factor, figured as $dt' = dt/(1 - v^2/c^2)^{1/2}$ – in which dt is the time that passes when you move at speed v, dt' when you stand still, and c is the speed of light. Thus the closer one approaches the speed of light, the slower time moves. Traveling at 80 percent of the speed of light for ten years would leave the astronaut four years younger than his brother. In other words, completely contrary to common experience, Einstein's formula suggests that time passes slower when you move extremely fast than when you sit stock still. At 80 percent of light speed, though, the flier could circle the equator six times a second, making one wonder what this might mean at more achievable speeds. Having little math myself, I asked a friend writing about time travel to calculate the Lorentz factor at a more reasonable speed, something a human being could actually do, but his calculator kept rounding off the number, leaving no discernible difference, for say, the twin flying at 500 mph jet speeds for ten years. If he could travel at 100,000 mph, or roughly four times faster than the fastest conveyance ever built (the interplanetary probe Pioneer 10), the twin would only be seven seconds younger than his brother after ten years. On United Airlines, he extrapolated, circling the globe nonstop for ten years would make the twin less than a hundredth of a second younger, and even if he was in first class we can safely assume that the ten years in flight would leave him looking much older. Time is relative, in other words, in this Einsteinian sense, but not so as you would notice.

But culturally relative, yes, we all seem to agree. We know that we in the West now live under clock time, commerce time, the time of machine production, the time of the commodity, what we might be tempted to call Franklinian time in honor of the man who first declared plainly that "time is money." Before this, over the long stretches of human history, we had instead the "cyclical time" of seasons and agricultural processes and growth-cycle-induced feast days: quasi-natural time. Modernity, the consensus has it, makes time "irreversible," leaving us at a historical remove from cyclical time: modern time replaces natural time. Modernity and postmodernity regularize and standardize time, Taylorize it, Fordize it and postFordize it, and thus devalue it. The more we accustom ourselves to a world of consumption and information, the more time becomes a particular kind of commodity. Instead of the "historical time lived by individuals and groups," according to Guy Debord, we postmoderns now experience time as

> an infinite accumulation of equivalent intervals. It is irreversible time made abstract: each segment must demonstrate by the clock its purely quantitative equality with all other segments. This time manifests nothing in its effective reality aside from its exchangeability... This is time devalued the complete inversion of time as "the sphere of human development." (19: Ch. 6, para. 147)

So sad. Manifesting nothing. And like the Einstein twins, so counterintuitive: from this perspective, the more that time is money, the more devalued it becomes.

Theodor Adorno explained this devaluation as a necessary concomitant of the "persisting conditions of unfreedom" of contemporary relations of production (Adorno, 1991: 188). Alienated from their own production, Adorno writes, workers are given chunks of free time that they then are encouraged to "use" to various ends, such as "do it yourself" schemes or even more vacuous projects like acquiring a sun tan. These meaningless activities devalue free time, just as being meaningless cogs in an industrial process devalues free time's opposite number, the working day. But there is an even wider cultural malaise afoot, he feels:

> It is also ... symptomatic of the deformations perpetrated upon man by the social totality, the most important of which is surely the defamation and atrophy of the imagination... Those who want to adapt must learn to curb their imagination... The lack of imagination which is cultivated and inculcated by society renders people helpless in their free time ... [because] that truncation of their imagination deprives them of the faculty which made the state of freedom pleasurable in the first place. People have been refused freedom, and its value belittled, for such a long time that now people no longer like it. (Adorno, 1991: 192)

Christ! What a world! Despite the internal contradictions of these arguments (the problem is that people can only think about time in terms of use value; the problem is that people make no use of their time), we can only affirm that, yes, we can see Adorno's plaint might describe some of what we experience. Since I see how this might be construed as a dialectic, maybe it's better to call it an affective contradiction, and one that we can all recognize: time is devalued by use and by uselessness, yes. We know both sides of this from experience – we have all filled out forms and we have all been bored. We don't have to agree with Sebastian De Grazia that under the regime of the work ethic "there is not much free time, nor likely to be much" (1962: 432–3) or with Debord in order to see that free time is not all we might want it to be.

But to see the devaluation of time as the result of some simulacral equivalence of time and money, to see it as simply an effect, a result of capitalist relations of production, is to obscure a deeper, longer history. Already in the third century BCE time was there to be spent. Theophrastus is said to have said: "Time is the most valuable thing a man can spend," and even in the medieval ban on usury we can find an acknowledgment that time is money. One cannot charge interest on late bills, a Franciscan lector-general explained in the fourteenth century, because in doing so the merchant would be selling time, and thereby "selling what does not belong to him." Time, according to this church official, belonged to God alone. The question here is not whether time is a commodity, simply a question of who owns it: in the late middle ages, as far as a lector-general is concerned, time is God's commodity.

Jacques Le Goff (1980) has described the dawning of "bourgeois time" in the twelfth through fourteenth century, charting the transition from "church time," with its emphasis on eternity and figuration, to "merchant time," with its emphasis on the time of labor, credit, and transportation instead. But in the late Middle Ages, he admits, these two forms of time didn't so much replace each other as peacefully coexist: "Natural time, professional time, and supernatural time," he writes, "were both essentially distinct and, at particular points, contingently similar," and this was not a case of medieval man's hypocrisy. "In different ways, the ends pursued in the distinct spheres of profit and salvation were equally legitimate for him" (Le Goff, 1980: 38).

Le Goff traces the various factors – Abelard's internalization of penitence, the rediscovery of Greek notions of time (cyclical rather than telic) through Arab manuscripts, Aquinas's understanding of Aristotle, confessional practices, socioeconomic changes – that helped construct a reevaluation of time by the fourteenth century. The wages of sin and the wages of work, we might say, were both being calculated and recalculated.

Max Weber's analysis of the relation between Christian and capitalist understandings of profit is thus given by Le Goff a slightly different genealogy. But in either case, whether we understand Protestantism as encouraging a profit-driven notion of time as Weber did or whether we see like Le Goff a more complex set of determinants constructing both Protestantism and money-time, it is clear that another couple of centuries later time was more like money than it had ever been. The religious folks who founded the Massachusetts Bay Colony, for instance, had a very clear sense of the correlation between time and profit. A colony law in 1633 announced that "No person, householder or other shall spend time idly or unprofitably" under penalties of up to a week's wages. "Misspending time" under this law could include "unprofitable fowling" or "tobacco taking" as well as loitering and drinking. This was bad news for loiterers, many of whom may have felt punished enough, since they had very likely been deported to the colonies for being loiterers in England. The colonies, eager for agricultural labor, cut deals with the City of London and others to take convicted idlers off their hands. Although Francis Bacon, among others, warned against sending "scum" to the colonies, John Locke was one of many who thought vagrants should be sent to America, and John Donne thought it a good way to "sweep your streets, and wash your doors from idle persons" (see Tom Lutz, 2006).

When the Massachusetts General Court decreed in 1633 that "all workmen shall work the whole day" on threat of punishment and attempted to fix wages low enough to require men to work longer hours, they were enforcing both religious and secular views of the dangers of idleness, and doing so in concert with the home counties. Whipping and fines were imposed for idleness in Plymouth Colony, in Connecticut, and in Rhode Island in the late seventeenth and early eighteenth century. Connecticut in 1750 had "An Act for Restraining, Correcting, Suppressing, and Punishing

Rogues, Vagabonds, Common Beggars and other Lewd, Idle, dissolute, Profane, and Disorderly Persons, and for setting them to Work." The ministers did what they could to help, as well; Benjamin Colman, a minister in Boston reminded his flock in 1717 that "All Nature is Industrious and every Creature about us diligent in their proper Work." Colman, John Cotton, Thomas Hooker, and Cotton Mather were, according to historian Paul Bernstein, "the last bastion of God-centered work values," and John Cotton preached that "cursed is he that doth the worke of the Lord negligently, and the work of the calling is, the worke of the Lord." Cotton Mather is said to have remarked about the unemployed: "Let them starve."

Mather was an important influence on Franklin, at first through his writings, and then through his scientific activities and his library, which he opened to Franklin as a young man. So it is no surprise that as Franklin secularized the work ethic and theorized time he retained many of the same basic values as Mather, including the distinction between the deserving and undeserving poor. The majority of important thinkers, writers, and politicians in the colonies and early republic agreed. Thomas Jefferson, Benjamin Rush, Richard Henry Lee, Samuel Adams, Henry Laurens, John Adams, Nathaniel Ames, John Pynchon, Samuel Johnson (the American Samuel Johnson), Samuel Willard, John Brainerd, Benjamin Wadsworth, and John Winthrop all extolled industry and decried idleness. They believed that giving charity to loiterers only increased begging and did nothing to help stem poverty. Boston therefore built a workhouse in 1685 for both the deserving poor and the criminals "who lived in idleness and tipplinge with great neglect of their callings." Almost a century later, in 1769, Boston commissioned and adopted a report on the condition of the poor that concluded that idleness is "the parent of all vices." Boston and Newport "warned" off vagrants in the 1720s and 1730s, and New York and Franklin's Philadelphia made a concerted effort to drive off vagrants in the 1760s. Wasting time was a crime.

In the context of this kind of fervent, widespread, and punitive embrace of time as money, Franklin's proverbs are notable not so much for their Weberian force as for their dose of irony. In fact it is hard not to read *The Way to Wealth*, his 1758 compilation of Poor Richard sayings, as deeply ironic:

Methinks I hear some of you say, *Must a Man afford himself no Leisure?* — I will tell thee, my Friend, what *Poor Richard* says, *Employ thy Time well if thou meanest to gain Leisure*; and, *since thou art not sure of a Minute, throw not away an Hour.* Leisure, is Time for doing something useful; this Leisure the diligent Man will obtain, but the lazy Man never; so that, as *Poor Richard* says, a *Life of Leisure and a Life of Laziness are two Things.* Do you imagine that Sloth will afford you more Comfort than Labour? No, for as *Poor Richard* says, *Trouble springs from Idleness, and grievous Toil from needless Ease.* Many without Labour, would live by their Wits only, but they break for want of Stock. Whereas Industry gives Comfort, and Plenty, and Respect: *Fly Pleasures, and they'll follow you. The diligent Spinner has a large Shift*; and *now I have a Sheep and a Cow, every Body bids me Good morrow*; all which is well said by *Poor Richard.*

This is not simply a moralistic brief for productive time. Sloth is no comfort, yes, but the life of leisure and the life of sloth are two different things, and the bantering tone ("now I have a Sheep and a Cow, and every Body bids me Good morrow") suggests that we should attend to the style as well as the substance, to see Franklin winking at us.

The *Way to Wealth* is a funny document structurally, as well. The fictional persona, Poor Richard, listens to the fictional Father Abraham, who speaks in this pastiche of the previously published sayings of Poor Richard; this double embedding allows Franklin to wink at the reader in a kind of mock modesty. Father Abraham is an old dodderer, a blowhard without an original thought in his head, and even Richard seems a bit worn down by what he calls Abraham's "harangue." Richard admits that although it tickled his vanity to hear himself so often quoted, it "must have tired any one else." More importantly, the people who listened, he notes somewhat abashedly, "approved the doctrine; and immediately did the contrary." This kind of ironic distance on his own doctrine makes sense, for Franklin himself spent enormous amounts of time on things that had nothing to do with Poor Richard's simple calculus, like his unprofitable electrical experiments and community service. At best these activities would produce profit only circuitously, and nothing in the *Way to Wealth* would explain the virtues involved.

If Franklin's wit and philanthropy put the lie to his famous work ethic, so did his habits. He became notorious in London in the 1760s for his daily "airbath," which consisted of lying uncovered and naked on a bed for an hour, a practice he claimed was good for one's health. And when John Adams joined Franklin as part of the American delegation in Paris in 1778, Adams was appalled by his relation to time.

> I found out that the business of our commission would never be done unless I did it... The life of Dr. Franklin was a scene of continual dissipation... It was late when he breakfasted, and as soon as breakfast was over, a crowd of carriages came to his levee ... some philosophers, academicians, and economists ... but by far the greater part were women... He came home at all hours from nine to twelve o'clock at night.

Adams reports that Franklin kept his constant dinner invitations carefully noted in a pocket hornbook, and "it was the only thing in which he was punctual." One of Franklin's French friends wrote that though Franklin indeed did do his work, "there never was a more leisurely man." Adams was more blunt: "He is too old, too infirm, too indolent and dissipated to be sufficient for the Discharge of all important Duties." In September the Congress disagreed, and brought Adams home, leaving Franklin as its sole representative in Paris, dismissing as well the other members of the delegation, men who had also complained of Franklin's laziness and his time-wasting ways, and carped that the only thing he wasn't late for was dinner.

In fact, Franklin himself wrote that it was more important to appear busy than to be busy. "I cannot boast of much success in acquiring the *reality* of this virtue," he writes of his attempts to be humble during his quest for moral perfection, "but I had a good deal with regard to the *appearance* of it." When he was first setting up as a printer as a young man he could see that "the industry visible to our neighbors began to give us character and credit" and after he was successful, he continued to make a show of his own industry, careful "to avoid all appearances to the contrary," pushing rolls of paper to his shop in a wheelbarrow down a busy street, and then having his workers to take over once he was in the door. Franklin's concern with the appearance of industry is like the early computer games that had a button to push so a graph would appear if the boss was coming, a stratagem, a simple, almost comic ruse. Time is money, and the saying is reversible: money is also time. And besides, as Franklin's own practice suggests, the maxims only go so far as descriptions of what we actually do, of how time actually feels. Time is not, after all, simply money. Certainly not time spent on an airbath.

On the other hand, perhaps it is self-serving of me to see Franklin as an ironist, since, as I have long suspected, I probably harbor an inadequate appreciation of the relation of time and money. As an adolescent and young man in the late 1960s and early 1970s, I lived under several different dispensations of time, however much I was, in all sorts of fundamental ways, as subject to the clock as the next person living in the postmodern industrialized world – I went to stores when they were open, I took scheduled transportation, I met people at prearranged times. But I was also at least partially convinced that some kind of Aquarianism was upon us – however quaint, if that's the word, it seems now – that a new cultural regime was ascendant, one that would mean the end of history as we had known it, and although I wasn't at all sure what that would mean, it affected my sense of time. As is true for many religionists, it made the actual time I was living in feel somewhat suspended, like I was awaiting the beginning of real time: as if some new timeclock and punchcard were about to be invented, I was just waiting idly until it was time to punch in (although, of course, the new age was not going to have any timeclocks – we were pretty sure of this.) And there was another kind of time, due to my serial and sometimes parallel consumption of pot, speed, coke, psychedelics, and booze, which meant that subjective time was extremely variable. After a serious shot of nitrous oxide what seems like an hours – long dream sequence, a novelistic unfolding of vivid events, can occur in what turns out to be a matter of a few seconds on the clock. Conversely, five or six clock-hours of bar-hopping during a night of cocaine snorting seem to happen within the equivalent duration of an anxious wait for a bus. As a result, my daily sense of time was erratic and fickle, as if time were itself capricious, undecided.

And my relation to work produced yet another kind of temporal mix. I spent a lot of time without a steady job – living off the land, collecting unemployment insurance, working odd jobs, and taking in a little bar band money – so that my time and income had little direct correlation. I had no schedule to keep, very few meetings to make, no watch to wear, almost never an alarm clock to set. This had the paradoxical effect of sometimes lengthening and sometimes shortening my experience of time – days could be very long, for instance, while years flew by.

My favorite joke in those days I first heard told by a friend named Robin Williams, who toured the country, and still does, with his wife Linda, as a singer-songwriter in the folk vein. It helped the delivery that he had a bit of a twang. He told the joke something like this:

One day a friend of mine, while sellin' life insurance door-to-door in farm country, walks up to a farm house, knocks on the door, and when a woman answers he says, "Hello, Ma'am, I was hoping to sell your husband some life insurance, is he to home?" She says well he is, but he's out back, feedin' the pigs. "Do you mind if go around back, then, to where he's feeding the pigs, and sell him some life insurance back there?" "Knock yerself out," she says.

So my friend goes around back and sees this farmer standing in his coveralls and tall rubber boots, in the middle of a paddock full of a hundred or so hefty, medium-sized pigs. In the middle of the paddock is an apple tree, and the farmer is holding up a 150 or 200-pound pig as it grabs an apple off the tree, crunches and swallows it, and then grabs another. [He imitates the pig hoggishly chomping through a couple of apples.] When that pig has its fill, he puts it down and picks up the next pig, aiming its snout at another hanging apple. The pig slops it down, and then another, crunches and slavers it, and the farmer lifts it up to get a higher one. Several apples later he puts that one down and picks up yet another pig, with a hundred more squealing and skittering, waiting their turns.

Now my friend could not believe his eyes, and he walks up to the fence and says to the farmer, "Listen, buddy, I've been sellin' life insurance in these parts for a while now, and I've seen a lot of farmers feedin' a lot of pigs, but I have never seen anyone ever, EVER, feed pigs anything like you're doing now." The farmer looks at him, says "Uh-huh," and picks up another pig.

"Seriously," my friend says, "People just do not feed pigs like this anywhere on God's green earth."

"Uh-huh."

"I mean seriously, don't you think that it's an incredible waste of time?"

The farmer thinks about this for a minute, and then says, scratching under the pig's ear: "Time?" he laughs. "What's time to a pig?"

This I thought was about the funniest thing I had ever heard.

I liked that joke, I have to assume, at least in part because it was a joke on me. I was living in farm country, raising some of my own food, cutting my own firewood for heat – the whole nine hippie yards. Like the farmer in the joke, I was wrapped up in natural processes and didn't calculate time the way a normal, normally enculturated modern person ought, and I was both proud of that and embarrassed by it. I knew that like the farmer, I was in part a naïve existentialist, a kind of organic relativist (to paraphrase Gramsci), and I also feared that I was at least in part just ridiculous, just a numbskull, living a little bit like an animal. And the life insurance salesman was my cultural opposite number: instead of natural, millennial time, the life insurance salesman deals in actuarial, modernist time, the time of risk, contracts, credit, and capital. Life insurance is a product related to the scarcity of actual time and is predicated on the fact that our time is not the same as other people's time; life insurance, assuming death, makes a bet about whether time will be shorter than we hope. But the joke is also on the salesman. His incomprehension sets up the reversal of perspective, to which he then falls victim. What is time to the capitalist pig?

Looking back at those years it seems remarkable to me that I could have assumed that time was as long as it was. Even though I was half convinced that I wouldn't live past thirty, my own death was always, nevertheless, in a very distant future. Now that I'm several decades closer to the event, and time continues to seem to go faster and to seem shorter (and I have a bit of life insurance), it still seems like it is fairly far off. The childish intimations of eternity – I think of the boy in Hemingway's "Indian Camp" who "felt quite sure that he would never die" – though, have been replaced with a slightly less grandiose conception of my own immortality.

So what is the point of this little excursus down memory lane? It is a way for me to wonder: what is the time of my life? I was raised in the New York suburbs: I knew nothing of agricultural time, I learned it only later. Oddly enough, at what might be considered the dawn of postmodernity, the very time of "the waning of the great modernist thematics of time and temporality," according to Frederic Jameson, the time when "our cultural language" became "dominated by categories of space rather than categories of time," (1991: 16) that I acquired a medieval temporal frame.

I moved forward from twentieth-century suburban time into traditional, pre-modern time, a time that has a surprising overlap with postmodern time. The postmodern, with its "overwhelming importance of the present" (Heise, 1997: 29), when "the present is all there is" (Harvey, 1990: 240), in dismissing modern, progressive teleologies, returns us to something akin to the cyclical time of the ages. Postmodern and pre-modern time privilege the timeless.

Still, as I experienced agricultural time, I no more lost my sense of clock time than the medieval lectors-general lost their sense of supernatural time when they came to understand time as a commodity. To experience working as a line cook in a very busy kitchen, or as an air traffic controller, is to experience time in a different way than a child at play in a sandbox, but we all know versions of all three. And as Bergson wrote, anyone can experience any number of different "rhythms": "In reality there is no one rhythm of duration; it is possible to imagine many different rhythms which, slower or faster, measure the degree of tension or relaxation of different kinds of consciousness and thereby fix their respective places in the scale of being" (Bergson, 1990: 207). New ways of talking about time can lead to new phenomenological experiences of time and vice versa, but my point is that we don't individually – and I'm suggesting that neither do we culturally – erase older ways of being temporal when we learn new ones. My panic at the shrinking, countable, sadly foreseeable time I have left in this mortal coil doesn't always, or even that often, alter the sense I have had since childhood of the endless future stretching out in front of me. Franklin's belief that time was money and his belief in leisure caused him no cognitive friction, any more than my sense of my "billable" rate is present when I am lost in a novel.

Ungleichzeitigkeit the Germans call it, or at least Ernst Bloch does: the non-synchronic, multiple, incommensurable yet coexisting layers of time that we live in. John Frow has suggested that Bloch's concept is politically responsive to the unequal order of our world, an alternative to both the hegemonic reliance on industrial modern time or the "shattering into a myriad of dispersed and local narratives" (Frow, 1997: 9–10) suggested by classic postmodernism. But I'm suggesting instead that not only is it true that, as Bloch says, "Not everyone occupies the same Now," but also that we all occupy many Nows. We all live under several dispensations of time; our culture of time is not serial, it's parallel, even, I would argue, cumulative. Perhaps information time – the time of what Alan Liu calls "informationalism" is, as Jameson and other theorists of postmodernism suggest, a kind of presentism, but that doesn't mean that we all live in the present (Liu, 2002: 74). We continue to acquire modern temporality ("*the paper is due on September 22*") and "Fall" may mean that the colors of clothing in our online catalogs is changing, but it also means that the leaves and the weather are changing as well, and we know what this means in ways similar to those of a medieval town dweller. We are not born into this world knowing what it means to be late, we have to learn it, and being late, it turns out, has only tangentially to do with the clock. Every time we learn a new way of talking about time, that, too, becomes part of our temporal repertoire. This is not simply a matter of acquiring more information, but, at least sometimes, it means assimilating new frames for information as well.

Both the universality of clock time and the subjectivity of temporality were institutionalized in the late nineteenth and early twentieth centuries. As Stephen Kern has pointed out, the standardization of time, the carving up of the world into uniform time zones, began to take hold when the US railroads adopted standard zones in 1883. This was followed the following year by the international Prime Meridian Conference in Washington and international standards were cemented at the Paris International Conference on Time in 1912. In this same period Oscar Wilde published *Picture of Dorian Gray* (1890), H. G. Wells *The Time Machine* (1895), and Proust *Remembrance of Things Past*, the first volume of which appeared in 1912; Bergson and William James published their first important philosophical speculations on time in 1889 and 1890, and the following years saw the scientific work of Lorentz and Einstein, the anthropological discovery of the relativity of time by Emile Durkheim and others, work on time perception in mental illness, and a new fascination with time in the visual arts (Kern, 1983: 12–35). For Kern, the fascination for these and many other writers is the relation of what he calls "public" and "private" time, clock time and subjective time. "The thrust of the age," he writes, "was to affirm the reality of private time against that of a single public time and to define its nature as heterogeneous, fluid, and reversible" (1983: 34). Kern suggests that it is precisely the force of industrial standardization that led intellectuals and artists, in reaction, however subconsciously, toward more fluid notions of time.

Certainly this makes sense for Durkheim, whose arguments for the relativity of time come after his conclusion that modernity leads to suicide. Durkheim's discovery of cyclical, primitive time, like mine, came from exposure to different cultures, but he was interested not in *Ungleichzeitigkeit* but in each culture's general relation to time, time as a general framework for culture, the relativism of official times. Philosophical arguments of this era – from James's notion of the "specious present" to Bergson's "duration" to Hans Reichenbach's reversibility to Heidegger's *Zeitlichkeit* assumed that something could be said about temporality in general, beyond its cultural specifics, including specific measuring devices like the clock. These arguments get most interesting when they reject any relation to the clock, not just through negation, as in the case of Reichenbach's speculations about time's arrow, but through resort to non-mechanical, non-material metaphors.

William James's notion of the "specious present," for instance: in his *Principles of Psychology*, he claimed that "the prototype of all conceived times is the specious present, the short duration of which we are immediately and incessantly sensible" (1950: 631) Later philosophers took issue with James's fuzziness on the issue, especially his somewhat lax definition of the relation between the "specious present" and duration: "We are constantly aware of a certain duration – the specious present – varying from a few seconds to probably not more than a minute, and this duration (with its content perceived as having one part earlier and another part later) is the original intuition of time" (James, 1950: 642). Bergson, at almost the same moment, developed his own notions of duration, in which clock time is irrelevant: "The duration lived by our consciousness is a duration with its own determined rhythm, a duration very different from the time of the physicist, which can store up, in a given interval, as great a number of phenomena as we please" (Bergson, 1990: 204). For Bergson, anything like measurement is imbued with the processes of perception and memory: "Our duration is not merely one instant following another; if it were, there would never be anything but the present – no prolonging of the past into the actual, no evolution, no concrete duration. Duration is the continuous progress of the past which gnaws into the future and which swells as it advances" (Bergson, 1911: 4). This swelling is growth through memory; memory, he insists, is not a repository, nor is it a faculty – it is our very character. As Gilles Deleuze has pointed out, for Bergson, there are two kinds of multiplicity, numerical multiplicity and the kind that Bergson understands as duration: "an internal multiplicity of succession, of fusion, of organization, of heterogeneity, of qualitative discrimination, or of *difference in kind*; it is a *virtual and continuous* multiplicity that cannot be reduced to numbers" (1991: 38). Temporalities, for Bergson, like memories, in fact *qua* memories, multiply. "My mental state, as it advances on the road of time is continually swelling with the duration which it accumulates, it goes on increasing – -rolling on itself, as a snowball on the snow" (Bergson, 1911: 12).

One can imagine an argument about commodity culture being made here – that time as accumulation is an argument that equates memory with capital. And maybe the same could be said of Heidegger: although obviously a critic of modernity's degradations, of the way industrial, technological culture reifies – and one who would become nauseous when he had to leave his country home to go into a city – he might also be seen as capitulating to standardized time by insisting on time as the horizon for understanding being. Like James and Bergson, he distinguished his sense of temporality from "vulgar concepts" or commonsense notions of time, but he nonetheless insisted on the foundational nature of time itself. At times he sounds like Durkheim: "Temporality (*Zeitlichkeit*) has different possibilities and different ways of temporalizing itself" (1962: 352). At other times he sounds more like the railroad: "Time is primordial as the temporalizing of temporality" (1962: 380). Poor Richard agreed, too, that time was primordial: "Dost thou love Life, then do not squander Time, for that's the Stuff Life is made of." Long before Debord, Sartre argued that "If Time is considered by itself, it immediately dissolves into an absolute multiplicity of instants which considered separately lose all temporal nature" (1966: 293), which, although it is not meant to inspire despair at postmodern, exchangeable meaninglessness like Debord, might be considered a kindred philosophical position. Many theories of time since Sartre also might be considered consumerist theories of time; Quentin Smith has called one group of them theorists of "solipsistic presentism" (2002: 119–36), yet another metaphor that can seem designed to describe postmodern consumer society.

All of these various temporalities are ours. And these: In *Journal of Evaluation in Clinical Practice*, Steven Buetow, citing Heidegger, suggests that, since patients hate sitting in the waiting room and are made unhappy by what they see as overhasty or otherwise too brief clinical consultations, clinicians should try to manipulate patients' sense of time in both spaces, "to accelerate, and thereby compress, waiting times, [and] to slow consultations in order to increase their perceived lengths" (2004: 21). After bringing out the heavy philosophical artillery, Buetow's suggestions are so trivial and contradictory that it is a favor not to mention them them in any detail. They have nothing to do with Lacan's "short session" or Freud's discussion of the time of the analytic session in relation to transference. Instead, Beutow suggests the clinician have nice furniture in the waiting room as a way to make the time pass faster there; if the session threatens to be so short that the patient will feel ripped off, Beutow suggests the clinician provide the patient with more elaborate, time-burning explanations of their condition. The patient is buying time and advice, but the greatest of these is time. In *American Behavioral Scientist*, Elaine Yakura suggests that the notion of "billable hours" helps to validate the charges made by computer consultants: "Billing practices ensure that consulting services have uniform value, even where the realities belie the uniformity." And the fact that time equals money is less a primordial fact than a symbolic, commercial accomplishment: "[T]he ability to maintain the appearance of value while hours are being amassed and cut by consultants ... is a symbolic accomplishment; the operation of the billing system helps to create and reinforce the meanings of time and uses of billables for the consultants and their clients" (2001: 10).

Time is money, in this world of ours, but in so many, and such manipulable ways, and from so many temporal perspectives, that it is hard to say what kind of regime the "time of the commodity" is. A German sociologist studying people like me – university professors – found that we had enough money, really, and enough status, but not enough time, and precisely not enough of the kind of time Adorno and De Grazia and a host of others would like us to have: *otium*, the leisure for art and learning (Mueller, 1967). I, however, don't quite experience it that way. When I was asked to write this essay, I knew there would be no money in it, and I clearly thought I would have the time for whatever modicum of art and learning would be involved. I thought about what kind of time I would have for it, and, typically for me, thought there would be plenty, since I would have finished a book manuscript before I started it (the book manuscript is still unfinished) and I didn't have any other articles on my plate (I've since agreed to two others). At this point in my career an article more or less makes no difference to my salary or ability to move, and I have a large advance check waiting when I hand in the book manuscript. Not only is the time I spent on this not money, it is keeping me from money. But it is, more or less, *otium*: I am using some of the time I have for speculation in the philosophical sense rather than the economic sense of the word.

Like anything else, such speculation can be pathologized, and part of my sense of my own relation to time, work, and money is exactly that: I understand it as pathological. In an article in the *Harvard Business Review* Steven Berglas counts the ways:

> Anyone who has ever managed people who abuse time – whether they are chronic procrastinators or individuals who work obsessively to meet deadlines weeks in advance – knows how disruptive they can be to a business's morale and operating efficiency. But lessons in time management will have no impact on these employees. That's because real time abuse results from psychological conflict that neither a workshop nor a manager's cajoling can cure. (2004: 90)

As I write this sentence, I should say, this essay is a little over two months late.

> Indeed, the time abuser's quarrel isn't even with time but rather with a brittle self-esteem and an unconscious fear of being evaluated and found wanting. This article describes four types of time abusers typically encountered in the workplace: Perfectionists are almost physically afraid of receiving feedback. Their work has to be "perfect," so they can increase their likelihood of earning a positive evaluation or at least avoid getting a negative one. (Berglas 2004: 90)

Yes, sometimes it feels like that. I would like this to be perfect. But there simply isn't enough time. I should have written it before the semester started.

Preemptives try to be in control by handing in work far earlier than they need to, making themselves unpopular and unavailable in the process. People pleasers commit to far too much work because they find it impossible to say no. Procrastinators make constant (and often reasonable-sounding) excuses to mask a fear of being found inadequate in their jobs. (Berglas 2004: 90)

I do all three.

Managing these four types of people can be challenging, since time abusers respond differently from most other employees to criticism and approval. Praising a procrastinator when he is on time, for instance, will only exacerbate the problem, because he will fear that your expectations are even higher than before. In fact, some time abusers, like the perfectionist, may need professional treatment. (Berglas 2004: 90)

Perhaps it's time for that. But in any case, it's time to send this article to the editors. I hate being late.

REFERENCES

Adorno, Theodor (1991), "Free Time," in *The Culture Industry: Selected Essays on Mass Culture*, ed. J. M. Bernstein. New York: Routledge.

Berglas, Steven (2004), "Chronic Time Abuse," *Harvard Business Review* 82 (6): 90–7.

Bergson, Henri (1911), *Creative Evolution*. New York: Henry Holt.

—— (1990), *Matter and Memory*. New York: Zone Books.

Buetow, Steven (2004), "Patient experience of time duration: strategies for 'slowing time' and 'accelerating time' in general practices," *Journal of Evaluation in Clinical Practice* 10 (1): 21–26.

Debord, Guy (1995), *Society of the Spectacle*, trans. Donald Nicholson-Smith. New York: Zone Books.

De Grazia, Sebastian (1962), *Of Time, Work and Leisure*. New York: Random House.

Deleuze, Gilles (1991), *Bergsonism*. New York, Zone Books.

Fabian, Johannes (1983), *Time and the Other: How Anthropology Makes Its Object*. New York: Columbia University Press.

Frow, John (1997), *Time and Commodity Culture: Essays in Cultural Theory and Postmodernity*. Oxford: Clarendon Press; New York: Oxford University Press.

Harvey, David (1990), *The Condition of Postmodernity*. Oxford: Blackwell.

Heidegger, Martin (1962), *Being and Time*, trans. E. Robinson and J. Macquarrie. New York: Harper.

Heise, Ursula (1997), *Chronoschisms: Time, Narrative, and Postmodernism*. Cambridge: Cambridge University Press.

James, William (1950), *The Principles of Psychology*, Vol. I. (Originally 1890) New York: Dover Publications, Inc.

Jameson, Frederic (1991), *Postmodernism, or, the Cultural Logic of Late Capitalism*. Durham, NC: Duke University Press.

Le Goff, Jacques (1980), *Time, Work, and Culture in the Middle Ages*, trans. Arthur Goldhammer. Chicago: University of Chicago Press.

Kern, Stephen (1983), *The Culture of Space and Time, 1880–1918*. Cambridge, MA: Harvard University Press.

Liu, Alan (2002), "The Future Literary: Literature and the Culture of Information," in Karen Newman, Jay Clayton and Marianne Hirsch (eds), *Time and the Literary*. New York: Routledge, pp. 61–100.

Lutz, Tom (2006), *Doing Nothing: A History of Loafers, Loungers, Slackers and Bums*. New York: Farrar, Strauss, Giroux/Northpoint.

Mueller, Ernst F. (1967), "Working Conditions of American University Professors," *Kölner Zeitschrift für Soziologie und Sozialpsychologie* 19 (1): 52–63.

Sartre, Jean-Paul (1966), *Being and Nothingness*, trans. Hazel Barnes. New York: Washington Square Press.

Smith, Quentin (2002), *Time, Reality, and Experience*. New York: Cambridge University Press.

Yakura, Elaine (2001), "Billables: The Valorization of Time in Consulting," *American Behavioral Scientist* 44 (7): 1076–95.

CHAPTER 4

Information Wants to be Consumed

R. L. Rutsky

Information wants to be free.

Stewart Brand, *The Media Lab*

Stewart Brand's notion that "Information wants to be free" quickly became one of the most celebrated, and often cited, slogans associated with the Internet and information technologies. Like all good slogans, it was both succinct and suggestive, which allowed it – as a bit of information itself – to be taken up and used in a variety of different contexts and arguments. In fact, as this slogan was appropriated and recontextualized, its meaning was inevitably transformed, sometimes in ways that bore little relation to Brand's original intent. Thus, the slogan took on a performative function, demonstrating in its very dissemination what was asserted in it: the tendency of information to move, to spread, to escape control. Indeed, for some, the slogan seemed to anticipate and affirm the idea that information can take on a kind of life of its own, with its own desires and agency. For others, it served as a concise statement of the antipathy within information technology circles to any restrictions on the "free flow" of information. Examining the multiple senses mobilized by this slogan can, therefore, help us to understand not only what informational "freedom" might mean, but also the processes by which information is "taken up" and "taken in" – in other words, the means by which information is consumed.

One reason that "information wants to be free" struck a chord with many involved in information technologies was that it seemed to propose an extension of the constitutional guarantees of free speech and a free press to the realm of computers and the Internet. Freedom of information, in this sense, implied the right of individuals to distribute information freely, unconstrained by governmental or other forms of censorship. In this context, it is useful to note that "freedom of information" had already been invoked in the Freedom of Information Act of 1966, and its subsequent revision in 1974, which provided mechanisms whereby secret government information could, under certain circumstances, be made public. The idea that information should be "free" or "open," rather than constrained by censorship or secrecy, has been one of the basic tenets of cybercultural ideology, and can be readily seen in that culture's romanticizing of the hacker, its aversion to closed source code, and its paranoia concerning governmental regulation. What is often forgotten, however, is the extent to which these ideas of informational freedom echo the ideals and the rhetoric of the free speech movement and of 1960s counterculture more generally.

The early partisans of computer and Internet culture were in fact steeped in California counterculture, often portraying themselves as revolutionaries, outlaws, and "freedom fighters" in opposition to big government and big corporations. In this regard, the famed Apple Computer "1984" commercial, casting the Apple Macintosh against the rigidity and uniformity of IBM's "Big Brother," was merely an exemplary instance of a prevailing attitude. Among those who have pointed to this linkage between cyberculture and counterculture is Stewart Brand himself. As Brand has noted, "The early hackers of the sixties were a subset of late beatnik/early hippie culture; they were longhairs, they were academic renegades, they spelled love l-u-v and read The Lord of the Rings and had a [worldview] that was absolutely the same as the Merry Pranksters' and all the rest of us world-savers" (Dery, 1996: 27). Brand was, in fact, a member of Ken Kesey's band of Merry Pranksters as well as the creator of that bible of counterculture, *The Whole Earth Catalog*, but he was also the author of one of the earliest articles about computer hacking, and would go on to found one of first and most storied online communities, the WELL (Whole Earth 'Lectric Link).

John Seabrook describes the WELL in terms that make its countercultural heritage clear:

The WELL had grown out of the 1970s back-to-the-land-through-technology idealism embodied by the Whole Earth Catalog. The basic idea was that by providing citizens with the technology to do more things for themselves – to grow their own food, make their own clothes, build their own wells, design their own solar-heating systems, and, now, make their own media – you could free people from their dependency on mass consumer products and corporate marketing… The WELL was a digital version of that idea. (1998: 147–8)

It was in the context of these notions of independence from "mass consumer products and corporate marketing" on the one hand, and from governmental and legal restrictions on the other, that the idea of informational freedom arose. Yet, although counterculture has often been associated with a vaguely anti-capitalist leftism, the premises of cyberculture were less anti-capitalist than populist. Thus, informational freedom has continued to be posed in populist terms, in opposition to the power of big government and large corporations to control information, to restrict access to it. Indeed, it is hardly accidental that the increasing popularity of conspiracy theories – fueled by anxiety about large, secretive organizations – has coincided almost exactly with the rise of "information culture." In the rhetoric of informational freedom, small is indeed beautiful, while "big" – whether it refers to IBM, Microsoft, or to the nation-state – is equated with rigidity, lack of access, and totalitarian control.

The "small is beautiful" movement, of course, focused on localism and decentralization, which were seen as inherently more open, more democratic modes of organization. This argument translated easily to modes of communication as well. Ithiel de Sola Pool, whose book *Technologies of Freedom: On Free Speech in an Electronic Age* heavily influenced Stewart Brand, summarized the value of decentralized, "free" communication: "Freedom is fostered when the means of communication are dispersed, decentralized, and easily available, as are printing presses or microcomputers. Central control is more likely when the means of communication are concentrated, monopolistic, and scarce, as are great networks" (Brand, 1987: 219).

From this perspective, personal computers and the Internet have been seen as inherently liberating precisely because of their ability to decentralize or disperse information. No longer concentrated in large, mainframe computers, controlled by massive, top-down organizations (whether private or governmental), information is spread across many locations, and is thus made freely available for the public to access and use. The very fact of information's dissemination is seen as inherently libratory. Once information has "gotten out" on the Internet, where anyone can freely access and copy it, it can no longer be "put back in the bottle" – contained, controlled, owned.

The metaphor of the bottle, of course, casts information in the role of a "genie" that, so long as it remains in its container, must serve its owner or master, but that when freed, can no longer be "put back," no longer owned or controlled. Here, information figuratively takes on a mind, and a life, of its own. After all, without having some form of life or agency, information could not "want" to be free. Yet, the bottle metaphor also suggests that information is inherently fluid. And indeed, informational freedom is commonly figured – as freedom often is – in terms of an unconstrained fluidity, whose destiny is to flow, to spread, to escape confinement, to go where it will. In what is itself one of the most widely disseminated essays on information in the age of the Internet, "Selling Wine Without Bottles: The Economy of Mind on the Global Net," John Perry Barlow has used precisely these figures to support his argument against legal strictures on the distribution and use of information. Equating information with ideas, Barlow attempts to distinguish the "free-flow" of ideas from the "fixing" of those ideas in physical forms, in "bottles":

> the rights of invention and authorship adhered to activities in the physical world. One didn't get paid for ideas but for the ability to deliver them into reality. For all practical purposes, the value was in the conveyance and not the thought conveyed.
>
> In other words, the bottle was protected, not the wine.
>
> Now, as information enters Cyberspace, the native home of Mind, these bottles are vanishing. With the advent of digitization, it is now possible to replace all previous information storage forms with one meta-bottle: complex – and highly liquid – patterns of ones and zeros...

Barlow's distinction between the fluidity of information and the physical "bottles" in which it is conveyed echoes the now familiar distinction between software and hardware. Unlike hardware, information itself has no "hard," physical presence; it cannot be grabbed, fixed, held in the way that a machine can. Instead, information is figured as soft, fluid, "highly liquid." It flows and spreads, passing around or through walls and borders that would contain its dissemination, its freedom. For Barlow, then, the freedom of information is based precisely on information's supposedly innate ability to escape constraints. Attempts to control the "free" flow of information are therefore doomed to failure: "Trying to stop the spread of a really robust piece of information is about as easy as keeping killer bees South of the Border. The stuff just leaks."

The idea that information is always subject to "leakage," that its fluidity cannot simply be bottled and sold, might lead one to presume that Barlow is also opposed to the restriction of informational flow implicit in the notion of "intellectual property." He does in fact argue that "along with the physical bottles in which intellectual property protection has resided, digital technology is also erasing the legal jurisdictions of the physical world, and replacing them with the unbounded and perhaps permanently lawless seas of Cyberspace." In contrasting the "lawless" fluidity of information to legal and physical restrictions of it, Barlow portrays information within the libratory, outsider mythology of 1960s counterculture. Free information is, in other words, cast as inherently subversive or anarchic, in much the same terms that the counterculture posed the freedom of the individual against legal and societal constraints. Like many advocates of "information culture," then, Barlow aligns informational freedom with the individual freedom idealized by countercultural ideology. This alignment of informational and individual freedom can be readily seen in the idealization of hackers as heroic "freedom fighters," working against authoritarian control of information and of individuals. Free, or decentralized, information is supposed, as de Sola Pool argues of communication technologies, to foster individual freedom, as opposed to a centralized control over both.

Yet, it is precisely the mythology of the outlaw hacker, of the individual who stands against a restrictive, controlling authority, that allows informational freedom to be equated with individual freedom. Thus, for example, many entrepreneurial technology companies have imagined themselves as rebels who, much as in Apple Computer's famed 1984 commercial, "fight the power" of industry goliaths and large governmental bureaucracies in order to set information free, to decentralize it and make it accessible to individual users. Ironically, this David-versus-Goliath rhetoric seems to persist even when these small entrepreneurs themselves grow into corporate technology giants. Thus, for example, the Microsoft Corporation continues to portray itself as if it were a small, rebel entrepreneur threatened by governmental regulations that restrict not only Microsoft's "freedom," but the freedom of information itself. Freedom of information comes to be seen in terms of entrepreneurial freedom, the freedom to own and ultimately profit from information. Here, the idealization of individual freedom that was endemic to countercultural liberalism has given way to a libertarian capitalism in which capitalist entrepreneurs become "freedom fighters" battling against governmental and legal strictures on information. According to this logic, the fluid, "lawless" space of information – a space that Barlow figures both in terms of "open seas" and the "wild west" – is free because it is private, because it lies beyond the bounds of governments and laws. Here, in other words, the space of information becomes synonymous with the space of the market itself. Freedom of information becomes indistinguishable from the free-flow of capital, from the so-called free market. Indeed, information is itself reconfigured in the image of capital.

The tendency to confuse the free flow of information with the flows of capital is widespread in debates over the freedom of information. And, to be sure, no one could deny that both capital and information have frequently been represented in terms of liquidity and flows, in terms of the ability to spread across boundaries, to disseminate and thus reproduce themselves. As with information, a certain dissemination and decentralization is crucial to the continued functioning of capital. Often, in fact, this decentralization has been portrayed as symptomatic of a historical shift from a modern, industrial capitalism to a postmodern, information-based capitalism. Thus, for example, Michael Hardt and Antonio Negri can argue that "the decentralization and global dispersal of productive processes and sites ... is characteristic of the postmodernization or informatization of the economy" (2000: 297).

Yet, despite the tendency to treat information as synonymous with capital, or as a postmodern version of capital, information and its dispersion differ in significant ways from "free" capital. Allowing capital the freedom to move across borders, to spread, does not mean that capital becomes more evenly distributed, more freely accessible. One cannot download capital as one might a bit of open-source software. While a certain dissemination may be necessary to the reproduction and expansion of capital, this dissemination does not mean that capital becomes free, at least not in the sense of being freely distributed, free for all to own, to access, to consume. Capital, in this sense, *does not want to be free.*

If, indeed, capital were to become subject to an unrestricted distribution and consumption, it would lose its status, its value, as capital. No matter how broadly or "freely" it is spread, capital must, by definition, preserve its value as capital, its status as property. In this sense, capital can never be freely dispersed, spent, consumed. If it is consumed, it disappears; it becomes lost as capital. Capital always demands *a return.* The movements of capital are inevitably circular, which is why the movements of capital are generally referred to not as dissemination, but as *circulation.* "Free capital" is not, then, simply a matter of freedom from governmental or other constraints on the decentralization or spread of capital; it is more a matter of a circulation in which capital inevitably returns – and pays a return – to its owners.

Capitalists, then, have an obvious interest in seeing information as a kind of capital, on which they can earn a return. The digitization or "informatization" of ever broader areas of culture and knowledge has allowed many information companies to extract previously unrealized value from a wide range of existing materials, from art to biogenetic data, from music to economic research. Digitization has, in other words, enabled various cultural products and forms of knowledge to be more easily commodified and consumed. It has also permitted the production of entirely new information-based commodities, from computer software to digital communications technologies. This informatization was epitomized in the shift, beginning in the 1980s, in which major producers of cultural commodities began to define themselves not as providers of books or movies or music, but as purveyors of software. Software – and indeed culture itself – was thus reconceived as informational "content," downloadable and transferable across a variety of media and technologies. The term "software" had the added advantage of emphasizing the corporately-owned, commodity status of the information involved. This content was intended, moreover, to be a largely disposable, consumable product: software, in this sense, was viewed as the razor blade of the information age, the commodity-form of information.

As many corporations have since discovered, however, digital information is unlike razor blades and other physical commodities – and, for that matter, capital itself – in one important respect: the ease with which it can be copied and spread. Information's reproducibility is what enables its fluidity, its tendency to proliferate, escape containment, and spread. Indeed, as Stewart Brand noted, it is precisely because of the ease with which it can be copied and distributed that information can be said to "want to be free." Yet, when Brand coined this phrase, he was not simply referring to freedom as opposed to constraint or control; he also meant free as opposed to expensive:

> Information wants to be free because it has become so cheap to distribute, copy, and recombine – too cheap to meter. It wants to be expensive because it can be immeasurably valuable to the recipient. That tension will not go away. It leads to endless wrenching debate about price, copyright, "intellectual property," and the moral rightness of casual distribution, because each round of new devices makes the tension worse, not better (1987: 202).

On the one hand, Brand observes information's tendency to replicate and spread freely, which makes information easily available. Because of this availability, information tends to become "free" in terms of its value as a commodity: "too cheap to meter." On the other hand, Brand suggests that information's value is also a function of its value to consumers. At first glance, the "tension" that Brand finds between "free" and "expensive" information may seem merely an attempt to apply classical economic concepts of supply and demand to the realm of information. Yet, what is evident, if not explicit, in Brand's argument is that information's value is not determined, as with material goods, at the level of its production, but through the reproductive, dispersive processes by which it is consumed. While the distribution and consumption of material goods in capitalism remains largely separate from its conditions of production, the reproduction of information is integral to its dissemination and consumption. Although information spreads, virus-like, through replication, this replication, as Walter Benjamin foresaw, involves a dispersion that allows images or data to be seen in different places, in different contexts (what Benjamin (1969) called "exhibition value"). It is, however, *only through the process of consumption* that this reproduction and dissemination of data can occur. Consumption, in short, is the means by which information, whether expensive or free, reproduces and spreads.

Information, in fact, depends upon consumption for its very existence. Without being consumed, it ceases to be information in any practical sense, becoming merely a static and inaccessible knowledge, an eternal and unreachable verity. Information is, by definition, consumable. It is less the case, then, that "information wants to be free" than that "information wants to be consumed."

This revised slogan points to an important change that has begun to take place in our notions of consumption and information. Watching a film, listening to a song, browsing a web page, or reading an academic essay has come to be seen as just as much a matter of consumption as buying a product. As culture, art, and knowledge have increasingly come to be seen as data, they can no longer be conceived (if they ever could) as existing outside of a commercial, consumable context. In an age of information, everything is supposed to be consumable; there is nothing outside of consumption. Critiques of consumption, for example, become just as much objects of consumption as they are analyses of it.

Of course, as many theorists of digital media have observed, the consumption of information differs significantly from the consumption of material products. Unlike commodities such as food or fuel, information does not simply disappear once it is consumed. Information may be consumed many times without being used up. Indeed, consumption, in and of itself, replicates and spreads information. Consuming information inevitably involves disseminating information. We see this process of dissemination everyday on the Internet, where the consumption of, for example, MP3 and other software files takes place through a process of copying that allows information to be transferred to different locations. Here, consumption has been redefined, becoming less a matter of accumulation, as it was with material commodities, than of distribution. This can be seen not only on the Internet, but throughout popular culture, where cultural data – in the form of images, sounds, and signs – is continually disseminated through the process of consumption.

The diffusion of information through consumption is, however, a highly ambivalent process. It often provokes, as Mark Poster has argued of the Internet, anxiety about the stability of national, ethnic, and personal identities (Poster, 2001: 101–28). Immersed in the flows of information, we often feel ourselves increasingly adrift, without the security of an essential identity that pre-exists our role as consumers. Our sense of ourselves as subjects seems to have become part of this proliferation of information, these flows of cultural consumption. In consuming, we find ourselves caught in these flows, carried along by the tides of data that increasingly surround us. For many, the encounter with this process of diffusion or dissemination proves a profoundly disorienting experience. It is, moreover, disorienting not only for consumers, but also for those who distribute information or cultural software. As the dissemination of music, of movies and television, of computer programs and video games continues to overflow their channels of distribution, they find themselves losing control over consumption. Indeed, their efforts to restrict the dissemination of the "software" that they presume to own are precisely a matter of regaining control over consumption's fluidity. From their perspective, this dissemination must, at all costs, be channeled, made secure, and, of course, made profitable. It must, as I suggested previously, be turned into a circulation, one that both returns and pays a return.

If capitalism attempts to restrict or re-circulate the consumption of information (or the dissemination that is inherent in this consumption), this circulation inevitably revolves around a particular, if imaginary, point: a center. This center, which served as a ground for consumption even before the rise of information culture, is the notion of a free and autonomous individual subject (which is also, as I noted previously, central to the idea of informational freedom). In consumer societies, consumption comes to be seen as a means of exercising personal freedom and personal (or consumer) choice. The very act of consuming, of making choices among consumable items, is viewed as an expression of our individual identities. We come, then, to recognize and define ourselves through our consumption, whether through the clothes that we buy and wear, the cars that we drive, or the films or websites or artworks that we choose to view. Here, the freedom of the autonomous subject has become synonymous with the freedom of the consumer. The consumer, in other words, is conceived precisely as a *consuming subject*, "free" to move and choose amongst the profusion of goods and software that seem to have been arrayed for his or her pleasure. Consumption, in other words, serves as a support for our sense of ourselves as autonomous individuals. It allows us to feel that we are choosing what and how we will consume, that we are in control of our lives.

This consuming subject can, in fact, be seen from the earliest stages of modern consumer society. Even in the nineteenth century, as Anne Friedberg has argued, consumption (of goods, signs, and cinema) constructed itself around the figure of a "mobilized, virtual gaze" (Friedberg, 1993: 29–40). Positioned to identify with this mobile gaze, the consumer-viewer emerged as a virtual subject, capable of moving, at least figuratively, through the dense profusion of goods, signs, and sights on display in the crowded arcades, department stores, and – somewhat later – the early cinema of the time. In thus positioning the consumer with (or as) a mobilized gaze, the unsettling density and dispersion of nineteenth-century urban life was translated into the personal mobility, autonomy, and freedom of a consuming subject. In an analogous way, the present-day World Wide Web gives users a similar sense of unrestricted mobility, autonomy, and vision. On the Web, the consuming subject is truly positioned as a mobilized, virtual gaze, freely navigating the "world" of information, consuming whatever strikes his or her fancy. The consuming subject's sense of mastery, of autonomy, of freedom, is thus preserved, shielded from the disorienting effects that might otherwise be provoked by the ever-increasing proliferation and dissemination of information.

Yet, it is not only the consumer who relies upon the figure of the autonomous subject to cope with the at times chaotic fluidity that is inherent in practices of information consumption. Those who provide and market information (and other goods) to consumers also tend to imagine themselves as subjects with identities and rights that must be maintained and protected against the dissemination of information. If copyrights and patents were originally designed to protect the rights of individual authors and inventors to their intellectual property, corporations have become the main custodians of these rights, buttressed by the legal fiction that corporations are individual subjects. Whatever value information may have to consumers, its value as a commodity – as software – depends on the ability of companies to control its dissemination, to channel its fluidity. Of course, the value of this information is determined not only by its content, but also by the relative speed with which it can be processed and distributed. Informational surplus value is not merely a function of having access to information, but of having access to it before others do. Whether this advance access is a matter of having the latest financial data before others or simply being the first on the block to have seen/heard the newest movie, music, or game, it serves to assert one's sense of distinction, taste, or style. The consumption of information, in other words, has become an increasingly important means of affirming one's unique identity, one's status as a free, autonomous subject. Indeed, information's ability to be tailored to fit one's interests has in fact led to an increasing ability to customize subjectivity, to customize ourselves. Thus, the consumption of information is less a matter of commodifying or fetishizing information than of fetishizing ourselves.

If, however, information's value is always relative to the consumer, this places even more importance on controlling its dissemination, restricting its flows to "authorized" channels. Such restrictions on the distribution of information seek not only to safeguard and maintain information's value, but to allow its consumption, like that of other commodities, to be metered and billed. Information therefore circulates within a restricted economy, in which returns accrue to those who distribute it. Distributors often imagine themselves as the subjects of this circulatory process, exerting control over it and reaping its rewards.

For both distributors and consumers, however, these efforts to define consumption as a process controlled or undertaken by autonomous subjects often seem on the verge of failure. The consumption of information is a vicious circulation. The more that distributors and consumers feel themselves overwhelmed by the proliferation and dispersion that consumption unleashes, the more desperately they try to redefine ourselves as subjects, to reassert their sense of mastery over consumption. Distributors, for example, find that their attempts to control informational flows continually go awry, overwhelmed by the vagaries of dissemination, copying, and piracy. Yet, as they employ increasingly frantic legal and technological strategies to make their information, and its value, secure, they also increase the value of unauthorized copies, thus promoting the "unauthorized" dissemination they sought to control. In a similar way, consumers discover that the more they rely on the freedom of consumer choice to define or "express" themselves, the more their sense of identity becomes lost, dispersed. If consumption promises to fulfill our needs, to improve our productivity, to make us feel more "complete," or "free," or "autonomous," it can only allow us to achieve these aims momentarily. Otherwise, there would be no need for us to continue consuming. We therefore find ourselves becoming consumption addicts, requiring ever-increasing doses of consumption — whether of goods or of information — simply to preserve our sense of being active, autonomous subjects.

While both distributors and consumers have a stake in presenting consumption as the expression of an active consumer's choice, the processes of consumption – especially the consumption of information – are not always amenable to choice or control. Consumption is not, in other words, simply under the control of a human subject. If, traditionally, critics of consumer society have sought to reassert the authority of a subject who would be independent of the system of consumption, the rise of information culture has made it increasingly obvious that there is no position where a subject might stand outside of consumption, even in order to critique it. Criticism positions us as consumers of information just as much as any other cultural product does. The consuming subject may be an imaginary construct, but this does not mean that an authentic subject (whether depicted in capitalist or Marxist terms) exists. So long as we continue to view consumption – and the entire world of information – in terms of this notion of a free, autonomous subject, we will remain caught within the vicious cycle that necessarily depicts consumption (and culture generally) solely in terms of whether or not it remains under human control.

To say, then, that information wants to be consumed is *not* simply a matter of saying that knowledge has, in an age of information, been reduced to a consumable, commodity status (the commodification of knowledge certainly pre-exists the rise of information). It is not simply "we" who desire and who consume. We are not the subject of consumption; we are, rather, consumption's medium, the means through which information manages to disseminate itself. Consumption is neither an action nor a course of action; it is a process in which we, sometimes without realizing it, participate. If we are to understand how consumption operates on and through us, we must attempt to rethink the concept of consumption, not in terms of subjects and objects, but as an interaction. We might, then, begin to imagine a consumption without consumers, which is not to say, without people, but without subjects as its end point. This notion of consumption would be defined not in instrumental terms, as a product of human needs and desires, but instead as an ongoing process with its own desires. Here, we might see consumption as similar to those turbulent processes in which an interaction of factors becomes too complex to be predicted or controlled. Indeed, the consumption of information has less in common with the directed, linear movements of intelligible "information" than with the fluid, chaotic dissemination of "noise." Like noise, the dissemination inherent in consumption conveys information, but that information is not necessarily conveyed to us. What we call consumption does not, therefore, exist because we choose to consume certain information, but because we cannot avoid it. If information wants to be consumed, disseminated, spread, we ourselves are inevitably part of that process.

REFERENCES

Barlow, John Perry (no date), "The Economy of Ideas: Selling Wine Without Bottles on the Global Net," Available online at: http://homes.eff.org/~barlow/EconomyOfIdeas.html (accessed March 30, 2005).

Benjamin, Walter (1969), "The Work of Art in the Age of Mechanical Reproduction," in *Illuminations*, ed. Hannah Arendt, trans. Harry Zohn. New York: Schocken Books, pp. 217–52.

Brand, Stewart (1987), *The Media Lab: Inventing the Future at M.I.T.* New York: Viking.

Dery, Mark (1996), *Escape Velocity*. New York: Grove Press.

Friedberg, Anne (1993), *Window Shopping: Cinema and the Postmodern*. Berkeley: University of California Press.

Hardt, Michael and Antonio Negri (2000), *Empire*. Cambridge, MA: Harvard University Press.

Pool, Ithiel de Sola (1983), *Technologies of Freedom*. Cambridge, MA: Belknap Press.

Poster, Mark (2001), *What's the Matter with the Internet*. Minneapolis: University of Minnesota Press.

Seabrook, John (1998), *Deeper: Adventures on the Net*. New York: Touchstone.

Part II

The Subject of Consumption in an Age of Information

CHAPTER 5

Consumer Discipline and the Work of Audiencing

Sean Cubitt

It hit me first when my power company changed hands. Among its assets it listed its customer base. In some far away boardoom, I was being traded. Of course it should come as no surprise to scholars of the media that customers are commodities. The economics of television has been understood in this way since the work of Dallas Smythe (1957): television sells audiences to advertisers – one of the first things we teach students in Mass Comm 101. Less clear however is the nature of the actual commodity being traded. The plural form "audiences" has become de rigeur, partly as a result of the de-massification of mass media over the last two or three decades. Yet even these target audiences have proved hard to observe as it were in the field. The commodity audience of market research seems harder to find at home or in the public spaces where, increasingly, targeted media operate. Ethnographers following the lead of David Morley (1980, 1987) have enjoyed the resistant play with media that they have observed, yet little of their evidence supports the economic argument which sustains advertising-led broadcasting. Most of all the "monkey see monkey do" theory on which commercials are supposed to operate is nowhere in evidence in the fieldwork. The old "influence" models persist among politicians anxious for a crusade, and lawyers whose defenses can always rest on precedents set when the community at large still believed in the efficient transfer of messages, rather than the negotiated terrain of meanings. In media studies the causal model of media effects is largely discredited.

It is also clear that the industry's concept of audience has changed. The undifferentiated viewer has become increasingly identified with lifestyles, aspirations, and subcultures, while the media have evolved to pinpoint highly specific micro-markets to accommodate the theory that consumers consume according to barely rational but nonetheless predictable patterns of interest and behavior. That this makes a mock of the mooted rationality of *homo economicus* is beside the point (it has never been a secret that economics is a profoundly ideological pseudo-science, specifically when it comes to the dogmatic application of theorems to policy initiatives). From broadcast to narrowcast to microcasting, marketing-driven media have been at pains to identify ever more specific lifestyle groups. But now that marketing defines itself as based on "mutually satisfying exchange," we have to begin to ask what it is that audiences exchange for their pleasures. It seems sensible to believe that whatever they may tell their clients, advertising agencies are not stupid enough to think they can influence behavior by putting commercials on TV or online. Besides, the chains of exchange between client, agency, medium, and audience are far more complex than a linear causal model could account for.

The theory of the information economy in its various forms posits the concept that data is of value, above and beyond the goods and services it once served. Much as finance capital has now subsumed and exceeded the older industrial and service sectors, so too the information sector has exceeded the boundaries of its predecessors. This does not imply that commodities are no longer produced, nor does it rely on the idea that brand identity is now a more valuable commodity than footwear or holidays. It simply argues that demographic data has become exactly what the Frankfurt School feared for American sociology – an instrumental knowledge in hock to capital. Contemporary audiences, however, receive programming, online content, and various media services in far more complex exchanges than can be accounted for in economic or marketing terms. Some of these exchanges are indeed monetary, as in the case of pay-per-view. Some are undoubtedly based on a willing or unconscious supply of data about lifestyle, interests, and purchasing (Elmer, 2004), but all are grounded in a shift in the kind of work that audiences do in return for programs, content and services.

Audiencing – the work that audiences do when they use media – takes place in a large-scale and complex industry involving content providers, service providers, account managers, media buyers, the marketing of media to agencies and of agencies to clients, all premised on the founding instance that audiences can be delivered to end-users. But just as a factory owner is scarcely interested in the complex lives of her hands, only in their labor, so the media industries are interested not in the cultural wealth of their audiences but in what they bring to the media business: their attention. What is bought and sold in the media market is not human beings. Slavery after all is illegal. What is bought and traded is the work of attending to media artefacts, specifically commercial ones. The media market is a market in attention. What media studies needs today is an attention theory of value to lay alongside Marx's labor theory. Audience attention, like factory labor, adds value to programs, channels, and portals. The attention so accrued, measured by the stickiness of websites as well as the sheer number of hits, the reach as well as the ratings of TV, and the priceless word-of-mouth generated in fan cultures, can then be traded through the chains of market researchers and advertising agencies, to product suppliers. Brand awareness and market share are the critical factors here: the ever-present possibility that the brand, should it lose its media presence, might fade away, effectively fading out of existence for lack of that attention whose supply the media industrialize. Here too there has been evolution, so that increasingly individual media products (*The Lord of the Rings* is a prime example) possess an identity that the brand (New Line Pictures in this instance) scarcely aspires to.

The industrialization of attention brings with it the proletarianization of consumption. The crucial factor here is the organization of viewing and using media. So much has been invested in developing and testing media services for their ability to target specific groups that nothing less than a fully disciplined work of audiencing will do. As the factory developed by the division of labor, so the media have developed with the division of audiencing. Generalized attention is of no more use to the contemporary media than generalized labor is to industrial capital. What are required are specialized skills in attending to specific media. Among these skills are knowledge of who you are and what you are supposed to enjoy. Those whose attention is neither specific not selective, who watch "television" rather than programs, and browse the magazine racks rather than read specific titles are less valuable: the elderly, the unemployed. But even these are significant sectors if individually a viewer or reader is able to turn their attention to specific use – as an opinion leader in a group for example. More valuable are those whose attention is more highly disciplined. The large audience among business leaders for tabloid newspapers is discounted; the smaller but more tractable audience for the financial press is a gold mine, whose attention is worth the immense amount of data put at their disposal in such publications. It is not simply the spending power of these audiences – every impoverished social science student reads the *Wall Street Journal* – as the quality of attention expended that valorizes the information or the entertainment offered. Attending to the "wrong" media is valueless in the commodity market for audiences. The audience for Cantonese pop among non-Chinese is not only economically marginal, it is insignificant in the sense that it is attending to an inappropriate medium. Its undisciplined attention is of no more use to the media market than tea-break football is to the factory manager, and quite possibly less so.

At the same time, media scholars have emphasized the activity of audiences not only in attending, but in creating meanings. These two perspectives on a single object – the activity of audiencing – one emphasizing the trade in attention, the other the production of meanings – have both been criticized in important work by John Hartley (1992) for presuming the existence of an audience or many audiences, that is, bodies of people assumed to be defined by their characteristic of being viewers (readers or consumers, active or otherwise). This public for media, whether considered consumers or manipulators of media, are determined in their relationship to media, and by their externality to the media system, as Luhmann (2000) would define it: the self-equilibrating economic, technological, and textual system that makes up the industry and its function within a larger aggregate, society, where it meets its audience. The audience exists then on the threshold between media and society, either as social entities engaged in appropriating media, or as economic agents translating media into social actions. Neither the possibility of integrating audiencing into the system of the media, nor the implications of such an integration for the conceptualization of both media and society have been fully explored.

To attempt this integration, I propose to move to a high level of abstraction. I take it that communication is a fundamental human activity, and that it takes place in material conditions such that communication is always mediated materially. This mediation engages three modes of materiality: physical, dimensional, and informational.

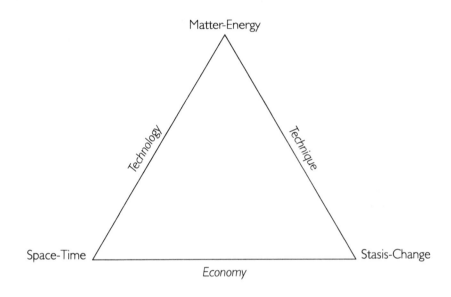

The material comprises the exchanges between matter and energy; the dimensional between space and time; and the informational between stasis and change. In the diagram above, the technological is seen as a mediation between physical and dimensional aspects of the media. Technique, the panoply of audiovisual and rhetorical devices that comprise the media as "texts", lies along the axis between the physical and the informational; and the economic is understood as a mediation between dimensionality and information processes. In this instance, the technical term "information" is to be understood in Bateson's definition: *"any difference which makes a difference in some later event"* (Bateson, 1973: 351). Bateson's example is the heat engine, where the available energy is defined as the difference between two temperatures. In the diagram, this difference is described as a polarity between stasis and change, where change can be either entropic or emergent. Thus technique manages the interactions between the physical properties, the matter and energy of the physical forms of, for example, filmstrips and broadcast signals, and their informational properties, notably their encouragement of maintaining or altering themselves, as in the modulation of novelty and familiarity familiar in both news media and popular music. Media technologies can be understood as mediating between the same physical properties of the media and their organization in space and time, for example in many-to-many communication via telecoms, or one-to-many live broadcasting, for example in multi-camera set-ups for live sporting events. The economic axis mediates between these spatio-temporal qualities and the informational, adjusting prices according to the speed and accuracy of delivery, and the distinctions between new and familiar which define the information content of messages according to their probability. The axes of technology, technique, and economy correspond to the familiar distinction between domains of the media apparatus: production, distribution, and audiencing, the gerund here flagging the activity involved in the attention theory of value.

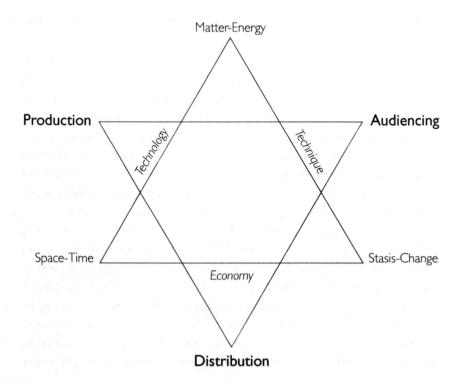

Production then corresponds to the familiar Marxist political economy of work. Commodities are produced as use-values which can then be exchanged and exchange-value extracted. Audiencing, as we have seen, belongs to the information economy, in which the labor of attention adds value to the commodity, and can therefore be defined as attention-value (as distinct, therefore, from Baudrillard's thesis concerning "sign-value"). Distribution lies between them, in the cycle of finance capital, thriving on the relation between exchange-value and attention-value to produce wealth by managing the dimensional-informational axis of distribution, the geographic and time-based control of flows and the rationing of relations, for example, between innovation and formula.

While these three sectors serve as analytical tools, there is clearly a great deal of interaction, so that for example the negotiations between audiencing and distribution around the equilibration of stasis and change have a very swift impact on production. Indeed it is extremely difficult to chart these relations as temporally distinct. *The Lord of the Rings* again gives a strong example. Pre-sales of distribution rights to overseas territories formed an important input into production even before the project was green-lighted at New Line; and from the inception, fan websites not only gave the producers and distributors a conduit for the drip-feed of promotional materials, but also had an impact on the production itself. Significant changes in any of the three domains of technology, technique, and economy will have significant impacts on all the others, most notably at present in the impact of digital networks on all three, a mutually reinforcing spiral of emergence. In other contexts, however, factors like the resurgence of Islam may resound sufficiently strongly in audiencing as to require reorientations of both production and distribution.

A critical question posed by the title of this collection concerns the interactions between consumption and information. Placing audiencing across the technique axis between physical and informational modes clearly associates it with the stasis-change aspect of media. Likewise, the emphasis in the preceding paragraph on the feedback loops between the three domains suggests that they can be read as integrated into a single system. However, it is not yet clear whether or to what extent production, distribution, and audiencing constitute distinct processes, and to what extent the media system as a whole functions as a system in informational terms. Put in the language proposed by Maturana and Varela, the question is whether the media system is autopoietic, and whether the embedded domains are in some degree autopoietic within it. Maturana and Varela's definition bears repeating in full:

> An autopoietic machine is a machine organized (defined as a unity) as a network of processes of production (transformation and destruction) of components that produces the components which: (i) through their interactions and transformations continuously regenerate and realize the network of processes (relations) that produce them; and (ii) constitute it (the machine) as a concrete unity in the space in which they (the components) exist by specifying the topological domain of its realization as such a network (Maturana & Varela, 1980: 79)

As opposed to allopoietic machines, whose function lies outside them – like a car, whose purpose has little to do with the car's internal states – living organisms, considered as autopoietic machines, have as their defining characteristic that they reproduce their own organizational structure. But for Maturana and Varela it is also an essential characteristic that the autopoietic machine is a unity, a unity that sure enough is reproducible as a unity by the unity itself (hence the *auto* prefix), but fundamentally a unity formed by a boundary distinguishing inside from outside.

Luhmann, drawing on this theoretical paradigm, is clear: the mass media (which he defines as the technological media that minimize or eliminate the interaction of senders and receivers) form an autopoietic system distinguishable, for example, from the political and economic systems on which they may report, but which they exclude from their own internal dynamic. Luhmann's argument rides on a proposition concerning the transition from the media system to the domain we are here calling audiencing: the three forms of mass communication he has singled out – news, advertising, and entertainment – converge in "creating the conditions for further communication *which do not themselves have to be communicated in the process*" (Luhmann, 2000: 65). That is, though the media system produces the themes and topics for dialogue outside the system, and provide the criteria for judging taste and being up-to-date, the conditions themselves are not communicated beyond the media system, which thus retains its autopoietic status as discrete, bounded, and self-sustaining.

Luhmann's persuasive and elegant argument against conceiving of the media as a machine in the service of politics or economics need not detain us here. What is significant is his characterization of the moment of audiencing as a boundary between systems. First given as a lecture in 1994, a matter of months after the release of Mosaic, the first freely-downloadable web browser, Luhmann's book can be forgiven what now appears to be an arbitrary distinction between mass and one-to-one or many-to-many media. That distinction was never strong, and has become weaker and more obviously so in the last decade, with the rise of the web, email, and mobile telephony, and their increasing integration into media networks. More important for the question of consumption in the age of information is the nature of the interchange between each of the domains. As we have seen, contemporary theories tend to place audiencing at the margin of the media system, more or less in agreement with Luhmann's assessment, if not with his analysis. Yet there is a sense in which audiencing is itself a mediation, a judgment fruitfully argued by Wolfgang Iser. Narrative fictions in many instances ask us for engagement not just in second guessing the action, but in making moral judgments and character assessments, issues that require an audience to interpret motives and outcomes as well as watching them unfold. Soap operas, detective fictions, and news coverage of political life all involve weighing our judgments of character and motive against both the unfolding narrative of events and the multiplicity of other interpreters and interpretations generated in the media system itself. For Iser, "The role of the reader emerges from this interplay of perspectives, for he finds himself called upon to mediate between them" (Iser, 1978: 33).

Each domain within the media system reproduces the cycle of the whole. In particular, the work of audiencing reproduces the cycle of production, distribution, and audiencing internally: this is the inference of Iser's term "mediate," a process that involves the whole nexus depicted in the diagrams above. This reproduction of the mediation process as a work of audiencing was clearer in earlier times, when entertainment and news required physical movement to special sites, places where a show would occur, or waiting for a special time, a season for mystery plays or carnival. The historical process that democratized access to spectacle on a daily basis, once the purview of princes, has also spread festival across the calendar. Yet some remnants of the spatio-temporal determinations of audiencing remain, for example in sport, even broadcast sport, where the cachet of live broadcasting is underwritten by the extra cash value often placed on it in terms of subscription to specialized channels. Where once the technologies of spectacle demanded an investment of time and traveling, now they require an investment in receiving equipment, a substantial sum acting as a hidden cost of consumption and part of the discipline required (like the factory system, where workers were expected to provide their own tools and uniforms). The dimensional aspect is also served by the embodiment of the viewer/reader, who grants the fleeting phantasms of the media the opportunity to come to some kind of flesh-and-blood existence. Without the work of audiencing, this embodiment, whether of advertising-sponsored desires or of thrills and chills from action adventures or tears for melodramas, takes neither place nor time. Embodiment, emphasized by phenomenological critics like Sobchack (1992, 1994) and Wilson (1993), serves also to give media artefacts and energies the object status they require, both to become meaningful and to enter into relations of exchange. And finally, in generating the conditions for dialog, which may be internal to a single person debating inwardly the interpretation of events, the mediation of Iser's reader involves sorting through the clouds of messages and apportioning significance. For information theory, this significance will be based on the probability of its occurrence, for a semiotician on the structuring of signs. Despite some sterling efforts, these two schools have yet to resolve their differences. Nonetheless, it is apparent that neither meaning nor signal inhere in the techniques of the media system. They belong properly to the work of audiencing, a work which, it becomes clear, must also be undertaken by all participants in the cycle, regardless of their position, if they are to assess what it is that they make or profit from.

The work of audiencing at the informational apex takes place about the dialectic of stasis and change. The autopoietic system is conceived as homeostatic: either a living organism maintains itself or it dies. In the years since Maturana and Varela, however, studies on emergent systems suggest that another possibility is open: the development of higher forms of order from apparently chaotic states. The media system is in a particularly difficult double bind. It must repeat itself if it is to maintain itself in a homeostatic state, but if it does nothing else, then it cannot produce information, only perfectly predictable patterns. It must therefore generate enough randomness to produce the effect of significance. The world can be relied on to provide a degree of randomness, but perversely not enough to satisfy the economics of distribution. By definition, the random is unpredictable, which means that it is not going to be available regularly or in the right places and times for production to work on it. This lack of reliable sources of randomness is often cited as the reason for the gradual abandonment of documentary as the prime genre of early cinema. Studio production, pulled along by the hunger of the proliferating nickelodeon boom, required a far steadier supply of events on film, resulting in the serial production of fictions, which made up in regularity of supply what they initially lacked in box-office draw. The informational apex (stasis–change) is referred to here as dialectical despite the fact that there are effectively three terms in play: entropy, homeostasis, and emergence. The words imply conflict, the sole stage in the triangle of physical – dimensional – informational where this can occur, and which therefore is the site of historical process in the media system. The topological aspect of autopoiesis refers to the dimensional aspect of this informational system, just as Maturana and Varela's term "component" refers to its physical aspect (and as they mention in a footnote, there are always energy costs to changes of informational states).

These distinctions are in some sense purely analytic, in that they are tools for the construction of a model of the media system. The virtue of this analytic model is less that it approximates more closely to the real of media, more that it runs counter to the findings of Luhmann, whose own tripartite division (news/current affairs, advertising, and entertainment) works generically without emphasizing the moment of consumption and therefore the problem of the transition between the media system and neighboring political, economic, and other functional systems that, in his analysis, comprise society. As a result, Luhmann's version reads the media as far more homeostatic than is in fact the case – a judgment based as much on the additional hindsight of the early twenty-first century as on any additional rigor in conceptualization.

The stasis change dialectic responds closely to the dimensional shifts identified by Virilio (for example in *Lost Dimension* 1991, originally published as *L'espace critique*), the diminishing of temporal and spatial depth through the acceleration of transport and communications, which have so profoundly altered the conditions not only of daily life but of the macropolitical conduct of globalization, and which, as Virilio's more recent work attests, continue to accelerate towards a genuinely homeostatic dimensionlessness (for example Virilio & Lotringer, 2002). This dimensional shift is largely experienced as informational by consumers, but as technological by producers, for whom the abbreviated feedback loops from market, critical, and fan indicators have become radically abbreviated, impacting directly on their sources and uses of energy and physical materials. At the same time, another analytic distinction – between analogue/photomechanical and digital/electronic technologies – would suggest that the analogue/digital distinction could be read as both cause and effect of both changes in technique and alterations in the economic moment of the media cycle. But then again, the economic itself has changed its dimensionality and its informational processes as a result of digitization, and the transformation of money from physical to electronic transaction, in other words its growing indistinguishability from the typical technological forms of mediation. So much so that Joseph Stiglitz can point out that a key reason why "markets do not work perfectly" is because of "asymmetries of information – the differences in information between, say, the worker and his employer, the lender and the borrower, the insurance company and the insured" (Stiglitz, 2002: xi).

One implication that needs to be spelt out is that money is now consumed, much as media are. Stiglitz's economics of information certainly suggests that the rich and powerful accrue and ration information, or at least benefit from its tendency to amass in certain institutions at certain levels, but it can also be seen as suggesting that the accrual of information is wealth, is power. Under the broader definition of communication that embraces all human interchange, economic flows are indistinguishable from transport or media. In the narrower field of technological media, seen in systemic perspective, wealth is generated in order to regenerate the cycle. Rather than an end in itself, e-money transfers around the triangle to purchase on the one hand new production, and on the other to buy consumers who can then be traded onward, as product, to such meta-consumers as advertising agencies and the clients that in turn consume the agencies' offerings. From the point of view of many, perhaps most, filmmakers and television producers, money is necessary in the first instance in order to make films and programs. Of course it is nice to make a living at the same time. But the vocation, in the strict sense of the word, of media maker is very largely driven by motives other than greed, and key rewards are status and critical acclaim rather than straightforward financial gain. Likewise, while most audiences understand their place in the economy of the mass media, as both purchasers of media infrastructure and media forms, and as the purchased good of the market in attention, the rewards they seek are rarely financial, and then often in such misleading forms as gambling, in any case a pursuit in which everyone knows they must bet against the bank.

The second aspect of the consumption of e-money is its informational structure. Individual units of currency are without information in the sense that one dollar is simply a repetition of another dollar. Sheer quantity of units becomes informational, but since there is a limit to the spending one person can do, that information has to be interpreted. In itself, wealth signifies little: it is only in the consumption of wealth as information that it approaches significance. At that juncture, it is comparison between sums that is interesting: a "difference that makes a difference" such as the cost of AIDS drugs relative to average incomes in different countries. This critical comparative interpretation is exemplary of the work required of the disciplined consumer whose ability to triangulate a given sum by both external comparisons and in relation to her own wealth provides both the normative functions that fascinate Luhmann and the resistances and psychic subterfuges that entrance the cultural studies tradition. More significantly still, the often-omitted last phrase of Bateson's definition is immensely important here: *"any difference which makes a difference in some later event."* The work of audiencing is critical not only to the maintenance of the system but to its overall evolution.

The act of becoming audience, of undertaking audiencing, is a surrender to a functional role inside a system that is otherwise than the individual. In varying degrees for various experiences of mass media, we offer ourselves as wholehearted or half-hearted *members* of an audience. In the case of complete immersion in a fictional (or for that matter documentary) diegesis, the extreme case taken as typical in apparatus theory (in the tradition of Christian Metz, 1982), audiencing has as its key task the recognition of the functionality of the media system. But in the distracted viewing of television or idle browsing through magazines and websites, dipping into the diegetic worlds on offer, and dipping out again (as in remote control channel zapping, but also in sharing conversations about programs) is far more of a boundary condition. While some aspects of contemporary media practice (digital broadcasting's offers of additional services parallel to the main program; use of websites, phone calls, credit card donations, and mobile text messaging) may appear to integrate telecommunications, print, and broadcasting, it is also the case that the intense competition for audience attention also disintegrates the media experience, now challenged to attend to many media, some – like computer games – clustered about the "home entertainment center," and some - popular fiction for example – leading away from it. If it is the case that narrative forms provide audiences with satisfyingly just, moral and logical, coherent experiences unlike those that constitute everyday life, and so provide consolation and/or utopian aspirations, what are we to say of these asymmetrical, dispersed, and distributed applications of attention?

The question concerns the changing nature of the media as a system. It is certainly possible to consider the media system, as a self-organizing autopoietic machine, as therefore capable of evolution. Indeed the problematic relation between innovation and formula, signal and noise, probability and randomness which constitute the informational apex of the cycle of media could be enough to generate change. Whether Luhmann's program types, technologically differentiated media forms or the moments of production, distribution, and audiencing, the components of the media system function neither discretely nor as a unity, but divided by times and places determined partly in the cycle of distribution, but very significantly in the work of audiencing.

The two moments are almost the obverse of one another. The economics of distribution concern control over the space and time of production, ensuring scarcity in the wealthiest markets and sufficient saturation of the poorest to ensure that no local centers of production can evolve in competition with the global players. Distribution then takes as its task delaying and rationing the flow of communication through the industrialized media. Its emphasis, we might say, is on its control over time, an orientation it shares with the financial markets, where trade in credit and debt is essentially temporal. At the same time, this de-emphasizes the spatial, which as a result is treated as both homogenous and unchanging. In the work of audiencing, however, place matters greatly. Local news, national sports, regional celebrities are immensely significant. But the progressive proletarianization of consumption results in a static time, in which all viewing, all browsing, feels to some extent the same. A product of the deferral of extra-systemic interests while paying attention to media, this approximates to the in-significance of units of e-money. The superfluous time that is destroyed in leisure is paradoxically timeless, its informational value ("that makes a difference in some later event") nullified: the probable source of that loss of depth, especially of historical depth, noted by Jameson (1991).

The informational content of audiencing then arises not from attention itself but from the constant oscillation of attention across the boundaries between components of the media system and across the boundary between the industrial media cycle and the rest of the communicative life-world. The work of consumption produces significance by working at the differences within media and between media and other communications – domestic, social, financial, political. Audiencing feeds back into the media system first and foremost the information that media are significant, in that they can interface with the other systems around them. More important at a formal level, however, is the consideration that the media cycle is dependent on this outward face, on the transit between inside and outside. The media cycle is not a closed system but profoundly porous, especially at the moment of audiencing, but also at every other stage of production and distribution. If it were not open, it would not be able to change.

A final theoretical point. It has been argued here that the choice of analytical models has an impact on how phenomena can be understood. These models cannot be dismissed for being mere abstractions, because they function in the self-understanding of systems like law (media effects), economics (the informed buyer), and politics (the literate citizen). Development of abstract models and debate concerning them is an integral part of the process of media history. The self-understanding of audiences who realize their economic and productive roles as well as their ethical and aesthetic tastes are part of contemporary citizenship. In particular, understanding that the work of consumption is work, and that therefore audiences have an effect on the media far stronger than the media's supposed effects on audiences, brings to the task of attending to media a sense of responsibility. The responsible citizen of a media democracy is not an end consumer, since audiencing transforms space, time, matter, and energy into information. This transformation is information because it makes a difference to later events, that is, it makes history. It does so specifically by failing to respect the borders between the media system, and the whole sphere of communication. The specific result of "consumption in the information age" is then to reproduce what was society as communication, specifically as mediation, the material transformations of the physical, and dimensional into the informational, both as structure, and as meaning. Such an understanding at once removes sociology's master problem, the relation of individuals, and society, and promotes the sense that agency is still a critical function in mediation.

REFERENCES

Bateson, Gregory (1973), *Steps to an Ecology of Mind: Collected Essays in Anthropology, Psychiatry, Evolution and Epistemology*. London: Paladin.

Elmer, Greg (2004), *Profiling Machines: Mapping the Personal Information Economy*. Cambridge, MA: MIT Press.

Hartley, John (1992), *The Politics of Pictures: The Creation of the Public in the Age of Popular Media*. London: Routledge.

Iser, Wolfgang (1978), *The Act of Reading*. Baltimore: Johns Hopkins University Press.

Jameson, Fredric (1991), *Postmodernism, or, The Cultural Logic of Late Capitalism*. London: Verso.

Luhmann, Niklas (2000), *The Reality of the Mass Media*, trans. Kathleen Cross. Stanford: Stanford University Press.

Maturana, Humberto R and Francisco Varela (1980), *Autopoesis and Cognition: The Realization of the Living*, (Boston Studies in the Philosophy of Science, Vol. 42). Dordrecht: D. Reidel.

Metz, Christian (1982), *Psychoanalysis and Cinema: The Imaginary Signifier*. London: Macmillan.

Morley, David (1980), *The "Nationwide" Audience*. London: BFI.

—— (1987), *Family Television: Cultural Power and Domestic Leisure*. London: Routledge.

Smythe, Dallas (1957), *The Structure and Policy of Electronic Communications*. Urbana: University of Illinois Press.

Sobchak, Vivian (1992), *The Address of the Eye: A Phenomenology of Film Experience*. Princeton: Princeton University Press.

Sobchack, Vivian (1994), "The Scene of the Screen: Envisioning Cinematic and Electronic 'Presence,'" in Hans Ulrich Gumbrecht and K. Ludwig Pfeiffer (eds), *Materialities of Communication*, trans. William Whobrey. Stanford, CA: Stanford University Press, pp. 83–106.

Stiglitz, Joseph (2002), *Globalization and its Discontents*. London: Penguin.

Virilio, Paul (1991), *Lost Dimension*, trans. Daniel Moshenberg. New York: Semiotext(e).

—— and Sylvère Lotringer (2002), *Crepuscular Dawn*, trans. Mike Taormina. New York: Semiotext(e).

Wilson, Tony (1993), *Watching Television: Hermeneutics, Reception and Popular Culture*. Cambridge: Polity.

CHAPTER 6

Sado-Monetarism, or Saint Fond-Saint Ford

James Wiltgen

In one of the most riveting opening passages in critical thought, Michel Foucault began *Discipline & Punish* with Damiens the regicide undergoing a rather radical and extended series of tortures before being drawn and quartered, as the strictures of sovereign society were inscribed on the social body. Foucault then points to the shift that occurred in a span of eighty years, with the rules decreed by Léon Faucher for young prisoners in Paris, what involved a series of articles for the orderly and coherent management of the actions of the State's charges; his argument revolves around the move from a public execution to timetables in terms of penal structures, and by extension the advent of what he terms disciplinary society (Foucault, 1977: 3–7). In an intriguing parallel to the torments of Damiens, N. Katherine Hayles begins the first chapter of her book *How We Became Posthuman* with a scenario taken from Hans Moravec, in which a robot surgeon extracts the mind of a human, uploading consciousness into a computer as a means of transferring the human into the machine, at least the "thinking" part, discarding the body and creating a new, perhaps posthuman entity who "resides" in the circuits of a computer network (Hayles, 1999: 1–2). What kind of shift do the forces propelling the world toward the downloading of consciousness hold for global society at this moment in time? In what ways might these forces be examined in terms of capitalism, subjectivity, consumption, and the political?

Obviously, cranial liposuction exists only as one possibility, one future that might be emerging given political, social, and technological configurations.

However, certainly Professor Hayles views the implications of this shift with studied trepidation, and her principal concern is the attempt to sever information from its location within human embodiment and the possibility of the body becoming a "fashion accessory" (Hayles, 1999: 5). Indeed, the key problem here resides in the conceptualization of information as what she terms the ultimate Platonic form, with all the dangers that implies, and this could mean an "erasure of embodiment" which she sees as beginning at the very dawn of the computer age. Hayles seeks to rethink, via the posthuman, the "articulation of humans with intelligent machines;" at stake here is not only embodiment, its enmeshed relationship to subjectivity, but the fate of the "liberal humanist subject" as she or he confronts a rapidly morphing present (Hayles, 1999: XI, 13). In other words, what agency will be charting the changes taking place along the full spectrum of shifts now occurring? Or, has agency already exceeded any human capacity, as systemic forces have already taken "control" of the forces of change. Hayles argues that given the potential for disastrous effects on the ecological and ontological stability of the planet "humans must be in control," that changes being made must maintain a "sedimented history incarnated in the body," and, because as she states in *The Eighth Day*, humans have become "biomedia created by the drive for domination and control," the following question must be posed, "(w)hen we become the objects of the domination as well as the subjects who enact it, who then is in control? (Hayles, 1999: 287, 280; Britton & Collins, 2003: 86).

MARKT ÜBER ALLES, ODER EXPERIMENTIEREN ÜBER ALLES?

On an analytical level, one of the ways to assess the changes taking place would be to see capitalism via the market as enacting a type of "enframing," where all of existence has been rendered into what Heidegger called *bestand*, standing reserve, as everything, *including the human*, lies within the purview of technological modernity. This current configuration of capitalism and modernity seeks to increasingly control all elements of existence, from the molecular to the cosmic, and with this power of control to organize

– basically in terms of fashioning more complex, as well as less complex organic and inorganic structures – the processes of the planet. In his book *The Will to Technology and the Culture of Nihilism*, Arthur Kroker argues that this enframing has been generated, in a dense series of feedback loops, by the emergence of Heidegger's concept of the will to will, the completion of a type of Nietzschean metaphysics, where the will to power sheds all embodiment and becomes a "pure will," folded back upon itself in a "recursive spiral" (Kroker, 2004: 123).[1] At one level, then, growing control by a logic generated via a rational and instrumental worldview, where the "governing" science, economics, uses a series of mathematical formulations to order all of existence; the market has come to replace, certainly in the West, the dominance of Christianity as a way of explaining as well as organizing the world (Bourdieu, 2003: 34). With the "death of God" as a signal marker, the changes in the psychological contours of the West, and by extension powerful elements throughout the globe with which it has resonances, would seem to be still in full process, or perhaps only in a mutating phase, or then again nearing its "end." Kroker definitely poses these questions, distilling Nietzsche with the query "what will succeed Christian nihilism?" and what happens when a culture … loses faith in representationality? (Kroker, 2004: 85, 165)

What would appear to have taken the place of Christianity, the basic "ground" upon which reality has been constructed, is the market – basically in its most tangible aspect as an ability to consume – both in an ontological and an ethical mode. As ontology, consumption provides the measure upon which the twin poles of the postchristian era, aggressive control and hedonistic boredom, receive their "philosophical" rationale, as both creative destruction and the "pursuit of happiness." On another level, and even more importantly, consumption provides the last, faint signal of a possible marker of salvation, because the ability to consume remains predicated in this schema on moral worth (in the most abstract sense, informed by a certain reactionary, radical materialism), which in turn points to the existence of God, or life, or the race – a type of transcendence – and on this basis acknowledges the possibility of "continuity," most particularly at the individual level, but for the more "perceptive" at higher levels of abstraction. Finally, as a correlative to the moral worth issue, a second means to interpret consumption holds that it represents the need for strong emotion, as a post-Weberian element of piety, demonstrating another type of "moral" character, one able to receive powerful emanations from the divine (see Campbell, 1989 and Slater, 1997). As an ethics, there is also a split – on the one hand, a neo-Darwinian imperative to select everything which enhances the power of the market, its propensity for consumption, and its continued deepening, while furthering the control mechanisms so many thinkers have analyzed, certainly with Marx being one of the earliest and most systematic. On the other hand, the unleashing of powerful new energies, both individual and systemic, provides the locus of one of the great paradoxes of the current moment. In other words, while an extremely cruel and powerful sociotechnological gird of organization has been and is being established, "counter" forces have also emerged, capable of trangressions, subversions, and resistances.[2] Enmeshed, then, in the "market" are other dense and complicated forces beside the so-called rational approach derived from the "objective" economic and mathematical models, ones inspired by a delirium and demented series of tendencies bent upon possible catastrophe, and perhaps the most sustained and pervasive forces of negation yet to be seen. In opposition to those forces, in some ways having developed "alongside" the delirium, one can detect new forms of subjectivity, capable of mutating the dementia in ways yet unknown but driven by tendencies of unrelenting affirmation.

One way in which to think the contemporary conjunction, then, might be to appropriate a term popular among various financial analysts and investment bankers in the early 1980s, namely "sado-monetarism." The two concepts, when joined, alter any analysis of the global situation, in particular calling into question the pervasive logic of "utilitarianism," including certain liberal and Marxist tendencies toward evaluating everything in terms of a "rationalized" approach, an instrumental reason if you will, based on a measured sense of profit and loss. In terms of analysis, this "profit and loss" must be complicated by the sub rosa forces driving change in the world order; in other words, the combination of *ressentiment* with utility, abuse-value with exchange-value (Kroker, 2004: 138). While the original use of the term demonstrates the Anglo-American biases of the commentators, coinciding as it did with the draconian cuts and restructurings of Reagan and Thatcher, its larger scope would be the vast and dense shifts the world economy began, if a date is necessary, when Nixon took the United States off the gold standard in 1972, and the speed of currency trade began to increase exponentially, paving the way for the explosion in finance capital of the 1980s and 1990s. At this point, various power coefficients that had been building within the global economy, among them the increasing impact of global corporations, the reach of market relations, economic and political strains on the nation-state, and the fluidity of currencies, began to have a more intense impact on the planet's organization. Now, in the early years of the twenty-first century, sado-monetarism might be interpreted in a number of different ways, including the continued, and by some estimates, growing immiseration of the world – mass poverty would seem to be a question not of production, where little doubt exists that enough food and shelter could be produced to enable the entire planet to have an adequate standard of living – but a matter of political will, or perhaps a dramatically different articulation of global economic and cultural systems. Is the fabled "permanent labor reserve" analyzed by Marx a structural element of capitalism, something the system needs in order to function, and without these "sacrifical" groups or "scapegoats" the system would collapse? Or, was the system constituted more by a certain "corrupted" will, the product of an ancient emergence, most powerfully marked by a Christianity in abeyance and ressentiment, and with this will a system of maliciousness and avowed avarice? Perhaps even more distressing, however one quantifies the developmental model being employed by the globe at this point, would be to question the entire growth model itself, based as it is on a rapacious consumption of the resources of the planet, driven by an unprecedented population surge that has more than doubled the world's inhabitants in the last forty years. One might ask what symptoms do these shifts signal, how and why have they occurred, and what possible courses of action do these nearly hallucinatory alterations close down as well as open up?[3]

Certainly the question "who benefits?" must be posed, and an initial response rests with a nuanced class and cultural analysis, providing not only an understanding of how wealth is appropriated but also foregrounding the issue of the creation of what Gramsci called a "hegemonic bloc." An analysis of this sort, the "monetarist" component, does function via a computation of utility employing a type of triumphant rationality, objectifying all of reality and reducing it to "standing reserve." At another level, however, what might be termed the "sado" element must be addressed, as extremely dense forces cut across the entire social and cultural system, including class, racial, gender, and ethnic lines, in feedback loops linking the macro-aggregates with the microtextures of production, antiproduction, consumption, and symbolic networks. As Deleuze and Guattari argue in their book *Anti-Oedipus*, with a decidedly Heideggerian echo, "there are no longer even any masters, but only slaves commanding other slaves;" (1983: 254). Baudrillard will pose the situation even more starkly, "humankind ... in its blind will for greater knowledge ... is sacrificing itself to an experimental destiny unknown to other species" (2001:33). In other words, control has been so densely embedded in the circuits of capitalism that it responds to events in a quasi-autonomous manner, a systemic configuration capable of fashioning actions in ways beyond the reach of even the most powerful groupings. Clarity here about this analysis remains crucial, as it does not seek to eliminate, or even discount agency and the possibilities of different articulations of the system, but to argue for the necessity of a multilayered approach, one capable of charting the power of a widely diverse and asymmetrical series of intertwined coordinates, from the political to the psychological, from the micro to the macro, or if you will from the molecular to the chaotic.

Another way to think the mutations of capitalism has been provided by Antonio Negri and Michael Hardt, where they argue that imperialism has ended and the planet has made a fundamental and irreversible shift into a different age, a new age of Empire. This new mode of global organization "is distributed in networks, through mobile and articulated mechanisms of control," which, although beginning in a Eurocentric context, now functions in global temporal and spatial coordinates (Hardt & Negri, 2000: XII, XIV, 384).[4]While the United States will maintain tremendous power in this configuration, it will not be the "center," but only serve as a powerful cluster of nodal points of control and organization; members of the G-8, factions of developing nations including China, India, Nigeria, Indonesia, and Brazil, to name a few, will also participate in the networked empire, where an adherence to capitalist logic provides the basis of global articulation and hegemony. With these changes a new sovereignty, a new subject has

famous homo faber takes center stage, as "man carries certainty of himself within himself". However, this formulation folds in upon itself, as the set of forces creating "homo faber" have now mutated, "redrawing" the measure, and contributing dramatically to uncertainty (Arendt, 1958: 279, 298). The form of measure has been set adrift, and the human now seems to be part of a vast "experiment" about which only tendencies can be discerned – as Leonard Cohen notes, "Though all the maps of blood and flesh are posted on the door, there's no one who has told us yet what Boogie Street is for" (2001). Arendt acknowledges this shift, this pervasiveness of doubt and uncertainty on the part of the human condition, and a "new zeal for making good in this life emerges," where "man can know only what he makes himself" (Arendt, 1958: 276, 293). The implications for consumption would seem quite clear in this analysis, as humans have been thrust back upon themselves, and the only reality possible in this scenario involves a radical and perhaps reactionary materialism, a passive/aggressive type of hedonism based upon production and consumption as the only criteria for "being alive." Or, as Arendt says, "the moderns needed the calculus of pleasure or the puritan moral bookkeeping of merits and transgressions to arrive at some illusory mathematical certainty of happiness or salvation" (1958: 310).

Baudrillard, in his later works, takes an even more "apocalyptic" stance to these shifts, asserting that the most pressing philosophical problem, uncertainty, has been generated because the contemporary world has extinguished its double, and there is no longer anything for which the world can be exchanged (Baudrillard, 2001: 3). The planet has entered what he calls the "ontological night," where *la pensée unique* or the concept of the "good," seeks to extinguish its opposite, but the good in this case seems to be at the "control of a suicide machine" (2001: 98, 15, 37,99). Due to this pervasive malaise, which might, if at all possible, be attributed to a certain "blind consumption … we are building a perfect clone," a "virtual technological artifact, so that the world can be exchanged for its artificial double" (2001L 99, 14, 28). He also argues that humankind, "in its blind will for greater knowledge … is sacrificing itself to an experimental destiny unknown to other species … in order to construct his immortal double" (2001: 33). This points to gathering forces of a "final solution" where the good has completely triumphed, the culmination of modernity's destruction of the world's double, so an artificial world may be put in its place, perhaps without leaving any traces. Consumption, in this very bleak landscape, furthers the construction of this artificial double, perhaps in order to pull up the ladder Wittgenstein speaks of, disappearing into another dimension, leaving this world and its "reality" behind. For Baudrillard, then, the absolute catastrophe would be for the total transparency of all data, a shimmering flash of everything in the now, initiating an implosion on the order of a second Big Bang. All this may seem somewhat hyperbolic, but then again cranial liposuction should, at certain levels, be taken quite seriously.

One possible response to this crisis of uncertainty would be to rethink the notion of wonder, what the Greeks referred to as *thaumazein*, that which depended, as has already been noted, on a sense of the "immortality" of the ancient world, or in another context, the "rational cosmos" of the pagans (Arendt, 1958: 233; Gillespie, 1995: 12). If one grants this argument for a moment, then what, if anything, might once again structure such a belief in the continuity of life? Jane Bennett, in her book *The Enchantment of Modern Life*, lays out a number of arguments that have been made for the "disenchantment" of modern life, a loss of the sense of wonder, beginning with Max Weber and continuing through a number of thinkers, including Hans Blumenberg; in place of disenchantment, she argues for a new form of "ataraxy", a new type of thinking the cosmos as Lucretius might have it — as a poetics to Venus, as a celestial harmony of the infinite swerve of atoms in the unfathomable expanse of the void. This intellectual maneuvering requires what might be called, in another context, a "leap," to think what Bennett calls "primordial harmony" (Bennett, 2001: 48, 140, 169). A way to transvalue Arendt's concept of "eternity," "repeating" it as a pagan belief in the continuity of existence, a way to "overcome" the pervasive and pernicious effects of ressentiment, and provide belief in this world. This would entail "an enchanted materiality," dependent on the primacy of connectivity over the encounter with the other, composed of the "primordially hybridized nature of everything" (Bennett,2001: 11, 80, 88). As politics, Bennett then calls for a much more careful analysis of all "goods" and their production/consumption, answering the questions what labor, what material, what profits, and what forces are involved; the stress here falls on what she labels, via William Connolly, as "inclusionary goods." Primordial harmony becomes the ontological basis of her approach, but the pivotal concept remains that of "shared materiality" as it provides the conceptual matrix to transvalue the entire structure of modernity and capitalism – the new assemblage would begin from a sense of a profound commonality, where all of existence encompasses the same molecular and material basis. Interconnectivity then would take precedence over alterity; affectivity would be the basis of an ethical/aesthetic approach to plentitude, and a cultivated sense of "generosity" would provide the abiding manifestation of this new sense of wonder. Bennett uses the work of Deleuze and Guattari as key thinkers in this reformulation, focusing on their sense of the positivity and affirmation of the world, as well as their call for the formation of a "new earth." Before addressing these issues, it will be necessary to take another look at the contemporary forces of capitalism.

WE HAVEN'T SEEN ANYTHING YET

How does digital capitalism intertwine with the concept of uncertainty? What key changes have taken place in the structuring of the world, via the digital and the biotechnological, what forces have emerged or coalesced, and finally, how do they affect the realm of subjectivity and consumption? Here, Arthur Kroker has transposed McLuhan into the twenty-first century, performing an interrogation of what he calls the "digital nerve," basically the exteriorization of the human sensorium into the digital circuitry of contemporary capitalism (Kroker, 2004: 81). This (in)formation, "streamed capitalism," rests not exclusively on exchange value, nor material goods, but something much more immaterial, – a postmarket, postbiological, postimage society where the driving force, the "will to will," has ushered in a world measured by probability. In other words, this variant of capitalism seeks to bind chaos by ever-increasing strictures, utilizing an axiomatic based on capture and control, with vast circuits of circulation as the primary digital architecture. This system runs on a densely articulated composition, similar to the earlier addressed concept of sado-monetarism, based upon extensive feedback loops running between exchange value and abuse value.

This assemblage, however, has multiple levels, and not all are connected to the grid at the same speeds; a number of different times exist within this formation, including digital time, urban time, quotidian time, transversal time, etc. Spatially, the structure relies not on geography but "strategic digital nodes" for the core of the system, and connectivity radiates out from these nodal points (Kroker, 2004: 125). For example, a key site for these points would be the Net corporation, defined as "as a self-regulating, self-reflexive platform of software intelligence providing a privileged portal into the digital universe" (Kroker, 2004: 140). Indeed, his mapping of digital capitalism has clear parallels with the shifts Katherine Hayles analyzes, in particular the underlying, driving mechanism whereby information severs itself from embodiment. Boredom and acquisitiveness become the principle markers of this new form of capitalism, which provides a rationale, or a new value set for the perpetual oscillation between the two poles, producing an insatiable desire for both objects and a continuing stream of fresh and intense experience.

Perhaps the most densely argued assessment of capitalism, whose obvious parallel would be Marx's *Capital*, is the two volumes by Deleuze and Guattari, *Anti-Oedipus* and *A Thousand Plateaus*. With all the concern over the theoretical concepts developed in these books, it remains extremely important to understand the analysis as possessing a fundamental focus on the question of political economy. Capitalism forms, via its structural and affective matrix, a system capable of unparalleled cruelty and terror, and even though certain indices of well being have increased, "exploitation grows constantly harsher, (and) lack is arranged in the most scientific ways" (Deleuze & Guattari, 1983: 373). Their framework for analysis targets the global, where the deepest law of capitalism sets limits and then repels those limits, a process well known as the concept of deterrorialization. Capitalism functions, then, by incessantly increasing the portion of constant capital, a deceptively concise formulation that has tremendous resonance for the organization of the planet—resources continually pour into the technological and machinic apparatus of capture and control, to the increased exclusion of the human component (Deleuze & Guattari, 1987: 466–7). In other words, it not only thrives on crisis but one of the principle definitions of capitalism would be to continually *induce* crisis; nostalgia for a "lost time" only drives these processes. The planet confronts the fourth danger, the most violent and destructive of tendencies, characterized as a *turning to destruction, abolition pure and simple, the passion of abolition* (Deleuze & Guattari, 1987: 229). Deleuze and Guattari make clear this fourth danger does not translate as a death drive, because for them desire is "always assembled," a creation and a composition; here the task of thinking becomes to address the processes of composition. The current assemblage, then, has mutated from its original organization of total war, which has been surpassed "toward a form of peace more terrifying still," the "peace of Terror or Survival" (Deleuze & Guattari, 1987: 433). Accordingly, the worldwide war machine has entered a postfascist phase, where Clausewitz has been dislocated, and this war machine now targets the entire world, its peoples and economies. An "unspecified enemy" becomes the continual feedback loop for this war machine, which had been originally constituted by states, but which has now shifted into a planetary, and perhaps interstellar mode, with a seemingly insatiable drive to organize insecurity, increase machinic enslavement, and produce a *"peace that technologically frees the unlimited material process of total war"* (Deleuze & Guattari, 1987: 467).[7]

Deleuze has analyzed these tendencies extensively in his own work, in particular with his dissection of active and reactive forces in his book on Nietzsche but also in his work on Sade and Masoch, where he points to a type of sadism that seems capable of attempting a "perpetually effective crime," to not only destroy (pro)creation but to prevent it from ever happening again, a total and perpetual destruction, one produced by a pervasive *odium fati*, a hatred of fate that seeks absolute revenge in destroying life and any possible recurrence. (Deleuze, 1989: 37). This tendency far outstrips what Robert Jay Lifton has described as the "Armageddonists," in their more commonly analyzed religious variant and in what he calls the secular type, both of which see the possibility of a "world cleansing," preparing the way for a new world order, be it religious or otherwise (Lifton, 1987: 5–9). Embedded within the immanence of capitalism, then, one can find forces which would make fascism seem like "child precursors," and Hitler's infamous Telegram 71 would be applied to all of existence, perpetually. (Deleuze & Guattari, 1987: 467). One final complication in terms of currently emerging subjectivities, the well-known analysis in *Anti-Oedipus* where capitalism, as basically driven by a certain fundamental insanity, oscillates between "two poles of delirium, one as the molecular schizophrenic line of escape, and the other as paranoiac molar investment" (Deleuze & Guattari, 1983: 315).[8] These two markers offer dramatically different possibilities for the issues of subjectivities and agency, and questions of consumption and the political can be posed within their dense and complex oscillations.

THE WASHINGTON SYNDROME AND THE RISE OF THE "DIVIDUALS"

During the latter stages of the Cold War, the United States and the Soviet Union effectively took the entire planet hostage, in the sense that questions of war and peace made by those two countries had the distinct possibility of ending global life as it has been commonly conceived. Indeed, after the advent of the hydrogen bomb, nuclear submarines, and MIRVed missiles, the destructive capacity of the two countries reached almost "mythical" proportions, producing what Helen Caldicott has called "nuclear madness" (2002), and Robert Jay Lifton has cited as a type of idolatry for what only god or the gods could do in the past, namely destroy the world (1987: 25). With the end of the Cold War, the United States emerged as the only "superpower," a "hyperpower" consolidating the destructive power of the world's most advanced war machine, and, responding to Nietzsche's question about who would have the will to become lords of the earth by responding: only those who would be willing to destroy it. In an intriguing twist on the course of theoretical formulations, the attempt by poststructuralism to undermine binary formations has, in a certain sense, come to pass – the "binary" division of the Cold War has been dissolved, but now the situation seems poised between a return to a type of unipolar formation, what Baudrillard called *le pensée unique*, or the advent of something more significantly dispersed and multiple. Strangely, large factions across the political spectrum remain nostalgic for the previous era of "stability," also known by the acronym MAD, mutually assured destruction. There is little doubt, however, that we have moved into another phase and another moment of dangerous intensity, where the stakes for global life continue to sway in the balance.

What has become abundantly clear involves the triumph of the US growth model, based on a neo-liberal approach, which seeks to marketize as much of the world's economy as necessary, with the exception of those areas the hegemonic powers deem crucial to exempt from those forces.[9] This dense and complex series of formations, or capitalism in another virulent manifestation, has been characterized by Deleuze and Guattari as "the age of cynicism, accompanied by a strange piety," where "capitalism's supreme goal is to produce lack," what they call "antiproduction" (Deleuze & Guattari, 1983: 225, 235). Two clarifications – first, cynicism corresponds to the notion used here of monetarism, an objectifying and quantifying of all existence, while the strange piety reverberates with a notion of "sadism," where the ressentiment produced by the "disappearance" of God, coupled with sexual, digital, and biotechnological mutations, drives capitalism, and where powerful tendencies within the system qua system would rather "will nothingness than will nothing at all."[10] Second, the production of lack has been set by the system itself, and the psychodynamics of the individual and the family have been generated from the macro-level, not the other way around. While one might grant complex feedback loops between the macro and the micro, the determining forces in this analysis stem from the aggregate level of capitalism itself. This lack induced by capitalism has produced a "quasi-infinite debt," where debt becomes the debt of existence, of life itself; however, it is important to note that there exist several types of debt, but the analysis here concerns the overarching one crystallized by relations of exchange, distilled and distorted by capitalism itself. (Deleuze & Guattari, 1983: 197). A new system of domination emerges, one generated by the mechanisms of the market and ressentiment, where confinement and discipline no longer form the key organizing principles of society, but debt, and where humans have begun the shift from individuals to "dividuals." In this society of control, digital and biotechnological modulations produce continuous vibrations, oscillating the human condition between forces of enslavement and what might be termed "other potentialities" (Deleuze, 1995: 178–82).

The American model, then, bases itself on a type of passive forgetting, which constantly configures the past into a self-justifying archive for the future expansion and manipulations of capitalism.[11] Again, this approach can be understood as the culmination of a long term dynamic, or as William Spanos argues, "the Occident has been essentially imperial since its origin in late Greek and especially Roman Antiquity" (Spanos, 1999: 3–5). Aggressive control of resources, the installation of market relations via debt, a political leadership offering "certainty," and the reduction of humans to cogs in a global matrix provide key elements of this model – the crucial question becomes: can it sustain itself, or has the model created an architecture of production and consumption which the planet and its resources cannot continue to supply? As one response, Heidegger might be paraphrased here, that "only a (technologically-beneficent) God can save us now." Obviously, these questions are far too dense to unravel here, but certain trends can be discerned. This situation will not be "solved" if American power goes into decline, as so many predict, because the basic tendencies have such tremendous resonance throughout the globe, with China and India being key examples in the processes of globalization. In Bataille's terms, the American-inspired variant of capitalism has perfected a restricted economy, and rather than expending some of the excess of energy in "profitless operations," they consume extensively, a type of reactive destruction, bent on a repetition for the sake of repetition, a repetition of the same, as the principle means of overcoming existential and political uncertainty (Bataille, 1988: 25).[12] What, indeed, is to be done?

"THINKING" ANEW

As has been argued, if capitalism consists of a plane of constructed tendencies, possessed of an axiomatics of immanence, how does this construction take place, what speeds and what coordinates are in play, and how can it be subjected to difference, or the repetition of difference? Capitalism has an isomorphic relationship to the virtual (basically Spinoza's concept of substance via Bergson), or the location of unlimited potentialities, but as a process of political actualization where these potentialities take on a materiality and a valence, but which maintain a constitutive split between the virtual and what becomes "actual." Agency remains possible in this interpretation as the politics of actualization, or the will to power, but a fundamentally different sense of the will to power as used by most commentators, from Nietzsche's contemporaries to Heidegger, and finally to Žižek. Deleuze altered dramatically Nietzsche's sense of the will to power, seeing it not as the culmination of the will to control, possess, dominate, or destroy, but as a relation of "creating and giving."[13] Thinking rests upon two different poles – on the vertical line, a sense of the virtual as pure speeds, as infinite movement; and on the horizontal plane, as the cultivation of both creating and giving. Deleuze and Guattari, in their final book *What is Philosophy?* have distilled a number of various strands into the central concept, arguably their last, and in many ways their most powerful thought-experiment, chaos. Here they use, as so often, a repetition of a previous formulation, one where earlier Deleuze had sought in some ways to "solve" one of the most difficult paradoxes of modern thought, namely to somehow reconcile Spinoza's concept of substance with Nietzsche's "machinery" of eternal recurrence. In *Logic of Sense*, Deleuze writes about a new synthesis, a more than cosmic composition, where the "univocity of Being merges with the positive use of the disjunctive synthesis," which is the highest affirmation, the so-called *event tantum* (1990: 178–80). Here, the merging of Spinoza and Nietzsche demonstrated one attempt to begin both a different genealogy and create the potential for a series of new fabulations. Chaos, then, as a political element, not simply the void but as infinite speeds with texture, as a thought-experiment that ceaselessly ungrounds, putting the basis of everything under the most nuanced of question and problem complexes. However, this chaos does not mean the seduction of nothingness, a desire to dissolve subjectivity; rather, chaos can heighten the capacity for thinking, a transversal capable of creating counterforces to those dynamics producing the sado-monetarist world.[14] Chaos as an ontological, or better post-ontological series of speeds, akin in some way to Lucretius and his sense of the void and those dazzling atoms; here, though, the sense of continuity, of certainty would seem to remain as a task, the problem of thinking in the most dense ways possible the concept of "discordant harmonies" (Deleuze, 1994: 146). Chaos vibrates between birth and death, raising them to the infinite as the two poles within which thought perpetually unravels, then ravels itself, not as a means to dissolve agency but as a means to create conditions for the emergence of the new. Thinking here seeks to generate a sense of consistency while not losing the connectivity to infinity, the manifestation of chaos (Deleuze & Guattari, 1994: 42, 118).

In the last chapter of *What is Philosophy?*, a more explicit connection has been made for the argument in this essay, namely the reciprocal predetermination of chaos and the will to power, now fashioned anew and "located" in the human brain. One might argue that chaos lies underneath, or behind the virtual, not as a transcendence but as the barely comprehensible phase of "infinite speeds" where an animate and expressive matter swerves in perpetual spirals. This void, this chaos meshes in some important ways with Jane Bennett's idea of plenitude, but here distinctions should also be drawn. Perhaps the most extended explication of the forces of destruction, of unraveling, takes place in Deleuze's *Difference & Repetition*, where the power of Thanatos, of unbinding, continually undoes form, a Dionysian force manifesting itself relentlessly in play and motion, ungrounding any configuration and creating new conditions for emergence. Deleuze calls these forces the "third synthesis," or the energy of chaos. Yet, the concept of reciprocal determination, of agency in the form of the will to power, pervades the work of Deleuze and that of Deleuze and Guattari, becoming the germinal binding which has a potential of creating the sense of wonder Bennett calls for.[15] Does the present moment have the requisite will to transmute chaos into wonder? Can chaos be enchanting? And if so, in what ways might a sense of generosity be induced in response to this quasi-incomprehensible concept? How might this alter patterns of subjectivity, including the contours of the object and patterns of consumption? Nietzsche projected his ideas in a two hundred year arc, and the planet finds itself just entering the second century of that arc. Does the world have the potential for a group of "new idiots" capable of creating and giving within a new thinking of chaos? Has the sado-aggressive will attained control of the strategic digital nodes of capitalism, and both evolution and the universe are being frozen in a perverted stasis, one of molar nihilism and a desire for cumulative and continuous destruction? Perhaps one of the only ways out would be to fold uncertainty back upon itself, by affirming all of chance, and to make "chaos an object of affirmation." (Deleuze, 1994: 243). Still, it might be too early to turn to new forms of plenitude, because the timing of any fold will be crucial (Deleuze, 1994: 65–6). Right now, parts of the planet function under the concept of "ubiquitous computing," where each individual is "shared" by a number of computers, tracked via the requisite algorithms of that database, giving a new twist to shared materiality as well as evoking another sense of bodies without organs (Kroker, 2004: 174). Consumption involves, then, a genealogy of the processes producing not only objects but relations among the extended fabric of reality; a fabulation regarding what onto-tales will be told about what exists; and a will to power reciprocally enmeshed in chaos, with the critical political task of producing a creative generosity. Perhaps, then, a limited sense of wonder might be possible, one concentrated on the nexus between the will to power as creating and giving and chaos as infinite speeds, enacted via natality and death, through the body (without organs), capable of releasing other forces, of crystallizing new forms and different relations. The key remains when and how to fold chaos, which may well be the task of our times. Gramsci put it very succinctly with a nice Nietzschean tonality: "pessimism of the intellect, optimism of the will," where the will becomes a "thinking anew."

NOTES

1. While there is not enough time to engage in a nuanced critique of this position, basically rereading Heidegger through Nietzsche rather than the other way around, Kroker's critique remains a powerful argument.
2. Gilles Deleuze (1995: 177), speaking of the new forms of control, "there's a conflict between the ways they free and enslave us."
3. See Gilles Deleuze (1987: 14), where he says "symptomatology is always a question of art" – this provides a continuing impetus for the present essay.
4. There is not enough time to deal with their other key concept, namely multitude, but it is fraught with a number of provocative problems.
5. Note the pre-Baudrillardian questioning of the nature of reality. Many will argue that this shift to uncertainty was "contained" in Christianity itself – see, for example, Bennett 2001, and her discussions of nominalism (2001: 66–72).

6. Corey Robin 2004, has argued that Arendt makes a crucial shift with her book on *Eichman in Jerusalem*, from total terror to the "banality of evil." While there is not enough time to engage with these arguments, the position of this essay is that there remain at least two levels of analysis, and the two poles form a type of continuum rather than a binary and fully oppositional construction. The same may be said for his distinction between the psychological and the political.

7. Chapters 13 and 14 in Deleuze and Guattari, upon a close reading, should dispel any doubts about the powerful analysis the authors make of contemporary political economy. As for some of the more dire assessments of current tendencies, the work of Dr Helen Caldicott (particularly 2002) and that of Robert Jay Lifton especially are recommended.

8. See also p. 376, where they argue that both poles involve "unconscious libidinal investments" – desire in this schema has been articulated within dense and complex political structures, and to understand patterns of consumption these articulations must be explored; see also 1987: 225, where they raise similar issues about why people might take part in their own "repression."

9. Michael Klare has argued that the Carter Doctrine of January 1980 laid the groundwork for both Gulf Wars. The doctrine stated that the U.S. viewed the continued flow of oil from the Gulf region as essential to its vital interests, and would use any means necessary to secure this objective. The argument in this essay, however, expands on the notion of resources, shifting focus to matters of geostrategic interests as well as ressentiment, and revenge.

10. See William Spanos (1999: 151), where he speaks of the Occident's dread of Nothing.

11. See Deleuze (1994: 55), for a discussion of "active forgetting."

12. Two examples of the notion of restricted economy: after the recent US elections, the next day an F-16 strafed an elementary school in New Jersey, and as this paper was being written, the US Marines were planning their largest single battle in Falluja, Iraq, since the Tet Offensive, 1968, Vietnam. The energy released by the US presidential election has been channeled into reactive destruction within a restrictive economy.

13. Deleuze (1983: pp. xii, in the Preface to the English Translation, & p. 84, where "'willing = creating' and 'willing = joy'" (vouloir = créer, volonté = joie p. 96, *Nietzsche et la philosophie*, PUF, 1962). In the second aspect, willing = joy, Deleuze seeks to increase the intensity of the "great Nietzsche-Spinoza equation," see Deleuze (1995).

14. See Gourgouris (2003: 140) for the cautionary notion of the *apolis*, "whoever thinks and acts alone," *Monos Phaonein*. Also see Luce Irigaray's *Marine Lover* for a very powerful reading of a type of *apolis*, which she misdirects, in large part, at Nietzsche.

15. See Deleuze and Guattari (1994: 42, 118). In this sense of individuation, in some senses they are stanch Cartesians, only they transvalue doubt via a Nietzschean affirmation.

16. Deleuze accuses Heidegger of "folding too soon."

REFERENCES

Arendt, Hannah (1958), *The Human Condition*, Chicago: The University of Chicago Press.

—— (1994), *Eichmann in Jerusalem: A Report on the Banality of Evil*. Harmondsworth, Middlesex; New York: Penguin Books, New Ed., 1994. First published: New York: Viking Press, 1963.

Bataille, Georges (1988), *The Accursed Share*, Vol. 1. New York: Zone Books.

Baudrillard, Jean (1993), *Transparency of Evil*. London & New York: Verso.

—— (2001), *Impossible Exchange*. London: Verso.

Bennett, Jane (2001), *The Enchantment of Modern Life*. Princeton: Princeton University Press.

Bourdieu, Pierre (1998), *Acts of Resistance*. New York & London: The New Press.

—— (2003), *Firing Back*. New York: The New Press.

Britton, Sheilah and Dan Collins (eds) (2003), *The Eighth Day: The Transgenetic Art of Eduardo Kac*. Institute for the Study of the Arts, Arizona State University.

Caldicott, Helen (2002), *The New Nuclear Danger*. New York: The New Press.

Campbell, C. (1989), *The Romantic Ethic and the Spirit of Modern Consumerism*. Oxford: Blackwell Press.

Cohen, Leonard (2001), *Ten New Songs*, Sony Music.

Deleuze, Gilles (1983), *Nietzsche and Philosophy*. The Athlone Press & Columbia University Press.

—— (1989), *Masochism*. New York: Zone Books.

—— (1990), *Logic of Sense*. Columbia University Press.

—— (1994), *Difference and Repetition*. New York: Columbia University Press.

—— (1995), *Negotiations*. New York: Columbia University Press.

—— and Felix Guattari (1983), *Anti-Oedipus*. Minneapolis: University of Minnesota Press.

—— and Felix Guattari (1987), *A Thousand Plateaus*. Minneapolis: University of Minnesota Press.

—— and Felix Guattari (1994), *What is Philosophy?* New York: Columbia University Press.

Foucault, Michel (1977), *Discipline and Punish*. New York: Vintage Books.

Gillespie, Michael Allen (1995)*Nihilism Before Nietzsche*, Chicago: University of Chicago Press.

Gourgouris, Stathis (2003), *Does Literature Think?* Stanford University Press.

Hardt, Michael and Antonio Negri (2000), *Empire*. Cambridge, MA: Harvard University Press.

Hayles, N. Katherine (1999), *How We Became Posthuman*. Chicago: University of Chicago Press.

Irigaray, Luce (1991), *Marine Lover of Friedrich Nietzsche*, tr. Gillian C. Gill. New York: Columbia University Press.

Klare, Michael T. (2004), *Blood and Oil*. New York: Metropolitan Books/ Henry Holt & Co.

Kroker, Arthur (2004), *The Will to Technology and the Culture of Nihilism*. Toronto, Buffalo, London: University of Toronto Press.

Lifton, Robert Jay (1987), *The Future of Immortality*. New York: Basic Books.

Robin, Corey (2004), *Fear*. Oxford: Oxford University Press.

Slater, Don (1997), *Consumer Culture and Modernity*. Cambridge: Polity Press.

Spanos, William (1999), *America's Shadow: An Anatomy of Empire*. Minneapolis: University of Minnesota Press.

CHAPTER 7

Closing the Net: "Capitalism as Religion"

Samuel Weber

Ein Zustand, der so ausweglos ist, ist verschuldend (A situation that is inextricable is guilt-producing.)

W. Benjamin, "Capitalism as Religion"

Was geschiehet, es sei alles gelegen Dir! (Whatever happens, let everything be laid out for you.)

F. Hölderlin, *Blödigkeit*

"We cannot draw closed the net in which we stand" – thus Walter Benjamin explains why he will not write an essay entitled "Capitalism as Religion." The text that bears this title, written in 1921, will remain a fragment, like Benjamin's "oeuvre" itself: a series of texts that never quite come together to form a work, but at most a "constellation" in which *empty spaces* are at least as significant as the "stars" they serve to situate. Benjamin's predilection for "Eternity by the Stars" – the title of memoirs written in prison by the revolutionary, Blanqui – which he saw as a precursor of Nietzsche's teaching of the "eternal return," did not exclude a certain fascination with more earthly structures and strictures: which is to say, with the knots and nodes, links and interstices that make up "the net in which we stand." This net will stretch in Benjamin's essay across the issues of the immediacy of information, the deification of number, and consumption as debt-as-guilt, to processes that entwine cult, capital, religious worship, fashion, and the consumer.

Yet, in Benjamin's text, this notion of standing "in" a net is curious. So curious indeed that the English translation prefers to replace "standing" with the more plausible, more familiar notion of being "caught": "We cannot draw closed the net in which we are caught" ("Capitalism," 288). What could be more convincing than being "caught" in a net? And yet, despite the fact that Benjamin *could* easily have written as much in German, where the word, *Verstrickung* stood ready and waiting to render the notion of being inextricably trapped, he chose instead to use the verb, *stand: "Wir können das Netz in dem wir stehen nicht zuziehen."* We cannot draw closed – draw to a close – the net, not because we are trapped in it, but because, more precisely, we are standing in it. We take our stand in the net. And not just in any net, of course, but in a particular one, the one for instance in which Benjamin sets out to assert, and argue, not just that capitalism is "conditioned" by religion, but that it *is a religion*, or rather, "an essentially religious phenomenon." Standing *in this* net, and at the same time *standing in for it*, Benjamin undertakes to develop an argument that the context, the "net," in which he and his readers stand, does not permit itself to be demonstrated.

The argument is simply, or not so simply, that capitalism must be considered a religion insofar as it "serves essentially the satisfaction of the same concerns, torments and troubles (*Sorgen, Qualen, Unruhen*) to which what is called religion formerly proposed answers" ("Kapitalismus," 100).

Just what these concerns, torments, and troubles in turn respond to, or address, will never be stated, not at least in this fragment. And perhaps for the very reason that Benjamin advances here at the outset of this text, and which explains why, in a certain sense, the text will never be written, or at least, never completely:

> The demonstration (*Nachweis*) of this religious structure of capitalism, not only as Weber believes, as a religiously conditioned phenomenon, would even today lead astray (*auf den Abweg*) into immeasurable, uncontrolled (*maßlosen*) universal polemics. ("Kapitalismus," 100/288)

In one of the very few references in his writings to Max Weber, Benjamin asserts the need to go further than the author of *The Protestant Ethic and the Spirit of Capitalism* in determining the significance of religion – and in particular of Christianity – for the socio-economic system that dominates the modern period. At the same time, however, he also asserts the impossibility, or rather, the *inopportuneness* of taking this very step, or at least, of *demonstrating* its necessity. Such a demonstration, the *Nachweis* that Capitalism is not just the result of a religious upheaval, but that it itself assumes the functions of a religion, would, Benjamin asserts, only lead to an incalculable and uncontrollable polemic. To provide a full-fledged demonstration that Capitalism "is" a religion, rather than being merely the result of one, would thus lead astray, along an *Abweg* that is precisely *off-target* by virtue of presenting *too many* targets. In a *Universalpolemik* everyone and everything is fair game, without limits or measure: *maßlos.*

The accomplishment of the project announced by the title of this short text, then, is rendered impossible, or inopportune, by "the net in which we stand" – we being the writer as well as his readers. Both stand in the net of a capitalism that, Benjamin asserts, *is* a religion, but, if it were named and above all shown to be such, would unleash a wave of aggression that, in its very limitlessness, could encompass the world.

The chilling and unusual word, *Universalpolemik*, echoes the more familiar *Universalgeschichte: universal history.* Except that what comes into view is not the culmination of world history, but the limitless perspective of a world at war with itself: a Hobbesian *bellum omnium contre omnes.* It is this prospect, however, by virtue of its lack of all measure, its *Maßlosigkeit*, that stops Benjamin in his tracks, as it were, here at the very outset of his argument. And yet, this most curious of all introductions still has one more unforeseen turn in reserve. After explaining why it is not opportune to offer a demonstration, a *Nachweis* of what therefore will have to be restricted to mere assertions, he concludes his opening paragraph, or gambit, with the following, rather cryptic prediction: "We cannot draw closed the net in which we stand. Later, however, this will be surveyed (*überblickt*)." Does this mean that the "net in which we stand" will "later" be drawn sufficiently to a close to allow us to look it over, taking it all in with our own two eyes? And just what is the "this" – *dies* – that is "later" to be surveyed? Is it the net? Our situation standing in it? The impossibility of drawing it to a close? The universal polemics its naming and exhibition would produce? All of these? Some of them? None? Something else?

As if this were not complicated enough, there is a second conundrum. Where are we to place this "later" that will bring the solution to which Benjamin refers? Is it simply further on in his text? Is it in a text written later by Benjamin (for instance, the *Passages*)? Or is it after Benjamin's texts as a whole, part of their "afterlife," perhaps including a situation in which "we" no longer "stand" in the same "net," or at least not in the same way? Could that *later* be today? Tomorrow? Yesterday?

Let us leave these questions in suspense, at least for now, in order to turn to another one that constitutes their common point of departure: Why should the demonstration that capitalism is a religion risk unleashing a global polemics defying all measure? A possible response is indicated by Benjamin's unusual choice of words. As already suggested, it is neither easy nor convenient to stand "in a net," especially when that net consists in "the same cares, torments and troubles" to which religion formerly provided answers, and to which today capitalism seeks to respond. What are those "cares, torments and troubles" and how does capitalism seek to respond to them?

Paradoxically, but significantly, it is the answer to the latter question that will allow Benjamin to approach, if not respond, to the former. It is paradoxical, since it amounts to inverting the usual, expected relation between response and that to which it is responding: stimulus, question, challenge, threat. It is no accident, however, that Benjamin takes the reverse route: he will first examine the nature of the response, in order then to approach, carefully, that to which it is responding.

Thus, after warning that he will not be able to demonstrate or bring proof of his assertion that Capitalism *is* a religion, and not just an effect of one, he goes on to describe what this assertion entails. Capitalism is a religion that displays four interrelated traits, all linked to the notions of *cult* and *guilt* (*debt-as-guilt*). These traits are, in the order followed by Benjamin:

1. Capitalism is a cult-religion, and indeed, perhaps "the most extreme that ever existed."
2. The cult of capitalism is extreme because it never pauses. It is characterized by "permanent duration."
3. The incessant cult of capitalism is *verschuldend*, which, according to the dual meaning of *Schuld* itself, must be translated both as "guilt-

producing" or "culpabilizing," and as "debt-producing" or "indebting."
In what follows, I will therefore translate *Schuld* as *debt-as-guilt*. And
finally,

4. The God of this religion, far from redeeming from guilt, is drawn
   into it. As a result, this God "must be kept secret and addressed only
   at the zenith of its (his) culpability-indebtedness" (*erst im Zenith seiner
   Verschuldung*)." ("Kapitalismus," 101/289)

Needless to add, these four traits, which are intricately intertwined,
demand discussion. To begin with, the relation of Capitalism to its cult
is, as we have seen, for Benjamin unique. If it is the "most extreme that
ever existed," this is not to be understood just quantitatively. Capitalism
carries the cult to the extreme in a number of ways. First, it frees the cult
from its traditional subservience to theological dogma, understood as a
series of ideas that would be exemplified or realized through the celebration
of rites. Rather, in Capitalism everything becomes meaningful only by
standing in direct, "unmediated relation to the cult." It is worth paying
particular attention in this phrase to the word "unmediated" or "immediate"
– *unmittelbar* – especially since it disappears in the English translation.[1] And
yet, as is often the case with Benjamin, a certain notion of "immediacy"
is decisive in articulating what is distinctive in his argumentation.[2] Indeed,
the entire question or problem of "Capitalism as Religion" hangs on this
nuance, namely, that it is not just a cult-religion, but a religion whose cult is
immediately meaningful. This *immediacy of the cult* marks the first in a series of
aspects that will distinguish Benjamin's notion of "cult" from the concept as
traditionally understood. Capitalism takes the cult to the extreme, Benjamin's
argument implies, by allowing it to become its own source of meaning, i.e.
by endowing it with a certain autonomy. As we shall see shortly, this radically
transforms its relation to the divine: instead of drawing its meaning from
the latter, or from ideas associated with it, the capitalist cult is itself the
locus and source of all meaning. But to attribute such autonomy to the cult
is at the very least to complicate the meaning of "cult" itself. Benjamin refers
to "Utilitarianism" in this context, suggesting that its "religious coloration"
can be illuminated through the notion of a cult that is itself the immediate
source of all meaning. Although he does not elaborate, one can surmise that
the immanence of the capitalist cult is related to a certain quantification,

or even a certain deification of number and of quantity ("the greatest good of the greatest number" being the phrase most commonly associated with "utilitarianism").

This suspicion could explain the transition from the first to the second trait of the capitalist cult: "With this concretion of the cult is connected a second trait of capitalism: the permanent duration of the cult." Since the cult no longer draws its meaning from something radically separate from it, but only from itself, that self consequently becomes its own measure. And the measure of a self is its ability to endure, which is to say, to withstand the transformative effects of time. This leads Benjamin to one of the most enigmatic lines in this text, if not in all of his writing. It is this: "Capitalism is the celebration of a cult sans rêve et sans merci" ("Kapitalismus," 100/288). Benjamin was, as is well known, fascinated with dreams. But his formulation here is startling all the same. For not only does it not seem to fit very well with what follows: it also echoes a French expression that means something quite different. The expression is, "sans trêve ni merci," "without *truce* or grace" (see Steiner, 1998: 156–7). It is a phrase Benjamin would have read in Baudelaire's poem, "Le crépuscule du soir," one of the *Tableaux Parisiens* that he had been translating for years and that he completed in the same year he wrote "Capitalism as Religion."[3] The phrase is decisive for the poem, which recounts how the evening twilight in Paris no longer functions as a refuge and consolation from the burdens of a day that for most is a work-day; for no sooner has the sun begun to set, then other figures begin to emerge to prey upon the unsuspecting. Those figures include

> ...les voleurs, qui n'ont ni trêve ni merci,
> Vont bientôt commencer leur travail, eux aussi,
> Et forcer doucement les portes et les caisses
> Pour vivre quelques jours et vêtir leurs maîtresses.

Although as Benjamin will demonstrate in his writings on the nineteenth century, dreams abound in capitalism and indeed are essential to it, what he here argues is that there is no "truce" or "pardon" in the capitalist work-day, which includes the night as well. Much later, in his notebooks for the *Passages*, Benjamin will observe that there is also no real "twilight" in Paris, because once the sun goes down the electric lights go on (J 64, 4). Even the natural alternation of day and night, then, tends to be suspended by the "progress" of technology. But in the text of 1921, it is above all the "cult" of capitalism with which Benjamin is concerned, and it is as "permanent" as it is revolutionary. But what it revolutionizes is above all the notion of cult itself. A cult is traditionally bound up with a spatio-temporally situated practice. As such it must be delimitable in space and time. That however is precisely what no longer holds of the cult of capitalism: it never stops, never pauses, never leaves room for "truce" or for "grace." It is, in short, permanent struggle and conflict that gives no quarter: "sans trêve ni merci." All that remains is "Schuld": debt-as-guilt. And, of course, the cult itself.

But if a cult is no longer consecrated to the worship of a deity that is by definition radically distinct from it, as infinite as the cult is finite, then just what sort of a "cult" is capitalism. And indeed, why call it a "cult" at all?

We have to remember that this text of Benjamin's dates from 1921, some fifteen years before he will invoke the notion of "cult" to distinguish traditional art from art in the age of its technological reproducibility. But as we shall see, the two "cults" have much in common.

The "celebration of the cult" in capitalism "knows no weekday" and hence, no *holidays* either. All days are equally holy: "No day that would not be a festive day" (a *Festtag*), but precisely because of this, the "unfolding of its sacral pomp" takes on a "fearful sense" (*einen fürchterlichen Sinne*), one involving "the most extreme exertion of the worshipper" (*der äußersten Anspannung des Verehrenden*).

We are far here from the "Feiertag" invoked by Hölderlin in his poem, "Wie wenn am Feiertage..." although the contrastive allusion is unmistakable, if implicit, in Benjamin's text. Why is this pompous celebration of the cult so *fürchterlich*, so horrendously fearful? After all, a demonstration of pomp is characteristic of traditional religious rituals, as is the "exertion" demanded of the worshipers? What is so fearful about the capitalist cult? "Wie wenn es keinen Feiertag mehr gibt?"

What happens then, quite simply, is that there is a war without end, *sans trêve ni merci*, a life-consuming exertion without truce or grace.[4] But if the war itself is without end, this is not true for the singular beings caught up in it, as the end of "La crépuscule du soir" makes clear:

C'est l'heure où les douleurs des maladies s'aigrissent!
La sombre Nuit les prend à la gorge; ils finissent
Leur destinée et vont vers le gouffre commun;
…Encore la plupart n'ont-ils jamais connu
La douceur du foyer et n'ont jamais vécu!

"Sans trêve ni merci," all there is at the end is "le gouffre commun," the common fate of singular mortals, many of whom have never known the comforts of home and indeed, who have scarcely lived.

But this grim ending in turn only poses a new question: how effective can the cult of capitalism be if this "gouffre commun" is all the "good news" it can bring in response to the "cares, torments and troubles" formerly answered by religion?

It is in answer to this implicit question that Benjamin abruptly, without explicit transition, moves to the third trait, which will turn out to be that which explains all the others:

> This cult is thirdly culpabilizing. Capitalism is presumably the first case of a religion that does not atone but produces guilt. In so doing, this system of religion stands in the collapse (*steht … im Sturz*) of an enormous movement. An enormously guilty conscience, which does not know how to atone, seizes on the cult, in order not to atone for its guilt but to make it universal, hammering it into consciousness until finally and above all God Himself is included in this guilt, so as finally to interest him in atonement. ("Kapitalismus," 100–I/288)

We begin to see why Benjamin began by noting that any "demonstration" – any *Nachweis* – of his argument would be extremely *inopportune* and would provoke a "universal polemics" with incalculable consequences. For it is never opportune to call attention to the fact that the net in which we are standing is drawn over the void. If this net cannot be drawn to a close, we now see why: the place "in" which we are standing is not just a net but also a "collapse" or a fall – a *Sturz*. Its "*enormous* movement" (*ungeheure Bewegung*) finds its equal and measure only in the "*enormously* guilty conscience" (*ungeheures Schuldbewußtsein*) that echoes it, but also momentarily suspends it as well. The "collapse" is a movement down to the earth and down into it, and as such is *ungeheuer*: excessively unfamiliar and yet all too familiar. Everyone takes this plunge because everyone is caught up in debt-as-guilt, *Schuld*. For the cult of capitalism, guilt is no longer limited to those who, like the ailing figures in "La crépuscule du soir," reach nightfall without ever having known daylight, but is extended to the universe at large, including its Creator.

It is here that the power and fascination of the capitalist cult begin to emerge. Its aim is not to secure Divine forgiveness or grace, but rather, in including God among the guilty, to "last until the end":

> It resides in the essence of this religious movement, which is capitalism, to hold out until the end, until the final and full culpabilizing of God, consummating the state of the world as despair (*Verzweiflung*) which precisely had been *hoped for*.

The only thing that presents itself as eternal in this world, is the cult of capitalism itself, which now takes over the role formerly assigned to the Creator, who has now become part and parcel of the Creation. As a result, the Creation is no longer the product and image of a transcendent divine essence – "God's transcendence has fallen," it "plunges" – but rather of an exclusive and ongoing process that brooks no alternatives and allows no way out. The formula for this achievement is quite simply that of "the extension of despair into a religious global system": *die Ausweitung der Verzweiflung zum religiösen Weltzustand*. The Creator is caught up in the headlong plunge of the Creation toward the abyss. There is no limit any more to despair, no escape from it.

In this process, the dimension of "globalization" is crucial. For it affirms the elimination of transcendence as the closing down of alternatives. "God is not dead, he has been given a human destiny." But that "destiny" only confirms a world in which there is no longer any way out. And it is this that seals the production of guilt:

> A situation that leaves no way out is guilt-producing. "Cares" are the index of this guilty consciousness of the lack of alternatives (*Ausweglosigkeit*).

The cult of capitalism thus does not merely *respond* to "cares, torment and troubles": it produces them, or rather reproduces them through its

elimination of alternatives, whether it be the transcendence of the divine
or an alternative social system. And what gives it its fearful efficacy, is that
it does not impose this reproduction from without, but rather from within,
through the consciousness of guilt, experienced not just as individual guilt,
but as a shared destiny of the community, *un gouffre commun*. In this way,
the consciousness of being guilty responds to, but also confirms, those
"cares, torments and troubles" to which religions have traditionally sought
to provide answers. If, as Benjamin writes, "Cares arise in the anxiety of
communal, not individual-material entrapment (*Ausweglosigkeit*)," then the
guilty consciousness fostered by the permanent cult of capitalism becomes
the basis of this communal experience, and the alleviation it presumably
affords.

But there is another aspect to Benjamin's discussion of capitalism as the
practice of an unremitting, guilt-producing cult, an aspect that we have
hitherto neglected, but that is indispensable to his argument. It has to do
with the fourth point, one that apparently occurred to him in the process
of writing, since at the outset he wrote of only three "traits" or features of
capitalism as religion. The fourth, as we have seen, has to do with the fate
of God. It also involves Benjamin in a discussion, on the border of criticism
and polemics, with two thinkers he cites by name: Freud and Nietzsche.

This fourth, unforeseen, and therefore supplementary "trait" (*Zug*), which
defines Capitalism as Religion and as cult, concerns its relation to its God. In
a passage that is strongly reminiscent of the Memoirs of Judge Daniel Paul
Schreber, but also of Nietzsche, Benjamin describes how the guilt-producing
cult of capitalism, far from seeking atonement from guilt, generates guilt
to the point where God himself is overtaken by it. "God is not dead," he
observes, but lives on as part and parcel of "human destiny," *Menschenschicksal.*
The notion of "Schicksal" — fate or destiny — had been a constant object
of reflection for Benjamin in the preceding years, culminating in an essay
published the same year that "Capitalism as Religion" was written, "Destiny
and Character" (*Schicksal und Charakter*). In that essay Benjamin sought to draw
a sharp distinction between the notion of destiny, which he associated with
a system of law and order (Recht) derived from Pagan myth and sustained
by "misfortune and guilt" (*Unglück und Schuld*) ("Schicksal," 174/203). Far
from breaking with the order of destiny, then, the legal system sustains and

confirms it. And it does so by addressing human beings as strictly natural, as "bare life":

> The judge can see destiny wherever he wants to: in every punishment he must blindly include destiny. The human being is never struck by this, but rather the bare life in him, which takes part in natural guilt and misfortune by virtue of phenomenality (*kraft des Scheins*). ("Schicksal," 175/204)

The "phenomenality" or "semblance" – *Schein* – to which Benjamin here refers is a result of the conception of human being as "bare" or "mere" life, which is to say, considered in terms of pure immanence. Only when the human being – *der Mensch* – is reduced to its purely natural and biological dimension, does it become *subject* to *destiny*, and hence to *guilt*. The paradox here is that human life, by being treated as though it were autonomous and self-contained, is inscribed in a nexus or network of guilt, a *Schuldzusammenhang*. What "holds together" the network is the refusal to accept a certain indebtedness qua relationality which is implied in the "naturalization" of human being as "mere" or "bare life." Cut off from its constitutive relation to others, the only other left to life is death. The hypostasis of life thus inevitably implies that of death. For life that is understand as merely natural, i.e. as "bare life," is rendered incapable of accounting for its constitutive condition, which is to say, for its finitude. The indebtedness to others thus is "internalized," rendered immanent, as "original sin," understood as the intrinsic cause of death. Death is thus interpreted as a product of life, of the Living, rather than as its enabling limit. *Schuld as indebtedness* is thus reinterpreted as moral culpability, as a *property* rather than as a *trait*. A property "belongs" to a subject and thereby stabilizes it; a *trait* tends to *draw it elsewhere*. As "guilt," *Schuld* seeks to define "bare life" in terms of itself: its actions and intentions, thus incorporating its "end" in its beginning. In so doing, however, it transforms the heterogeneity of human being into its absolute other and seeks to appropriate it as such. "Destiny" is the name of this appropriation, and the guilt-nexus is its medium. "Bare life" is thus inextricably linked to bare death. As *semblance*, "bare life" is thus inevitably haunted by its other, the shadow of a death that both *defines and exposes* its "bareness," its *Blöße*.

This is why something as little natural, as social and technical as a system of jurisprudence could become the institutional condition under which the semblance of "bare life" would perpetuate itself beyond the demise of the pagan religious system that initially supported it. It is in this context that Benjamin observes that

> Law (*Das Recht*) condemns not to punishment but to guilt. Destiny is the guilt-nexus (*Schuldzusammenhang*) of the living. ("Schicksal," 175/204)

When, therefore, Benjamin writes in "Capitalism as Religion" that God has been involved (*einbezogen*) in "human destiny," this is another way of saying that the divine is now enmeshed in the network of guilt that marks the medium of the living, as "bare life." But this introduces an enormous problem. For the destiny of "bare life," in being guilty, is to be punished by death. In this sense, the guilt of the living confirms death as the penalty for human existence. Death becomes a sentence punishing the living for the guilt of "bare life," i.e. of life construed in terms of the immanence of nature. In a note jotted down several years earlier, in the summer of 1918, Benjamin formulated the thought underlying this argument succinctly:

> Wherever there are pagan religions, there are concepts of natural guilt. Life is somehow always guilty, its punishment: death.

> One form of natural guilt that of sexuality, involving enjoyment and the generation of life.

> Another that of money, involving the mere possibility (*bloße Möglichkeit*) of existing. (*GS* VI, 56)

These three assertions help circumscribe the very complex situation in which the divine finds itself in the cultic religion of capitalism. First, the divine, by becoming human, has also become guilty of that "bare life" which is punishable by death. The only thing that survives is the guilt- and debt-producing cult of capitalism itself. But this cult in turn requires at the very least agents of appropriation and exchange: exchange of commodities, appropriation of value. Benjamin does not refer to this here, although he will much later, in his notebooks of the 1930s, the "Arcades Project." But he does already insist on the need for a certain figure of the human in order for the cultic system to function. It is a human figure that is deified precisely to the extent that the traditional religious deity has been humanized. But since this humanization of the deity also deprives the latter of its transcendence, the figure must be "hidden," but in being hidden, also elevated above the level of mere mortals. I quote Benjamin once again, describing this fourth trait of capitalism as religious cult:

> Its fourth trait is, that its God must be kept secret (*verheimlicht*), and only addressed (*angesprochen*) at the zenith of its culpabilization (*Verschuldung*: also indebtedness). The cult is celebrated before an immature (*ungereiften*) deity, each representation, each thought of it violates (*verletzt*) the mystery (*Geheimnis*) of its maturity (*Reife*).

To describe the deity worshiped by the cult of capitalism in terms of "ripeness" or "maturity" is to underscore what results when the transcendence of the divine has been naturalized and humanized. As human, the God is incomplete, but its incompleteness can only be construed in the terms of the living as "mere life," which is to say, as a lack of "maturation," as *Unreife*. This is why the naturalized–humanized God has to be kept secret, *verheimlicht*. But at the same time, given its integration into human destiny, the process of divine maturation can be construed only as the culmination of the guilty indebtedness of "bare life" to death. It is this that constitutes the "zenith" at which point alone it can be addressed, *angesprochen*.

The result is a cult that is highly ambivalent and ambiguous. It is designed to cultivate nothing other than *itself*, which is to say, its own ability to "hold out until the end." This cult, in short, cultivates the end as it own. It seeks to appropriate the end. But to do this it has to assume the appearance of the "bare" and barren "life" it both presupposes and seeks to outlast. The deity must therefore be hidden, and yet still be accessible – *ansprechbar* – so that the semblance (*Schein*) of "bare life" can be sustained. Life can be construed as bare only in the shadow of a semblance that cannot be seen and that in this concealment serves as an invisible object of adoration.

One way of worshiping such a concealed God consists in re-enacting the process of concealment. Such reenactment can take the form of *targeting*:

an object (person, figure, idea) is evoked, named, described, but only in order then to be done away with, sidelined, *beseitigt*. Perhaps this is why, immediately following his unforeseen description of the fourth trait of capitalism, the concealment of an unripe god, Benjamin takes aim at two targets, two proper names. The first is that of Freud:

> Freudian theory also belongs to the priestly domination of this cult. It is conceived in a thoroughly capitalist manner. The repressed, the sinful representation, is – by virtue of a profound analogy, yet to be thought through-capital, which pays interest on the hell of the unconscious. ("Kapitalismus," 101/289)

Benjamin takes aim at "Freudian theory," which he sees as participating in "the priestly domination of this cult" of capitalism. If psychoanalysts are priests of this cult, it is by virtue of a "profound analogy" linking "the repressed" to "capital." Although he does not develop this analogy, he associates it with the interest-bearing function of capital, which he assimilates to the repression of a "sinful representation." It is thus the theological, and for Benjamin essentially Christian notion of "sin" that provides the tertium comparationis, or, as Marx might have said, the "universal equivalent" for the "profound analogy" between capital and repression. Without being able to "think through" this "profound analogy" here, two points in Benjamin's account of it can be noted. First, he correctly describes the object of repression as a *representation* (*Vorstellung*), and second, he characterizes it as "sinful" – *sündig*. The representation is not "sinful," however, insofar as it is "an idea of sin," the curiously puritanical interpretation of the English translation. For the representation is "sinful" not because of its object, but because it claims to represent something that cannot be represented. Whether this is construed in Marxian (and Ricardian) terms as the socially necessary labor-time that constitutes the measure of "value," or whether it is conceived in religious terms, as a deity whose transcendent alterity defies representation, Benjamin's text does not say. By comparing the destiny of the repressed representation in the unconscious with that of capital, producing interest out of "the hell of the unconscious," Benjamin seems to imply that the debt- and guilt-producing "sin" of both – repression and capital – resides in the process of *self-production* that allows only quantitative and incremental distinctions. In the following paragraphs, where he is no longer criticizing Freud but rather Nietzsche, he will define the "function of guilt/debt" in its "demonic ambiguity" as that of *returning* "interest upon compound interest" (*Zins und Zinseszins*). The interest in a profitable *return of interest* is what transforms *Schuld* as *debt* into *Schuld* as *guilt*.

It is this self-consistency and continuity that also marks the second "target of opportunity" that Benjamin will cite, or take aim at, in order to instantiate or exemplify "capitalist religious thinking" – Nietzsche. The name, Nietzsche, enters Benjamin's text explicitly only to be negated: God is *not* dead, Benjamin writes, but rather lives on in human, natural form. Benjamin thus seeks to distance himself from Nietzsche at the same time that he acknowledges implicitly his indebtedness to the latter's pioneering analysis of the "demonic distinction" between *Schuld* as *debt* and as *guilt*. Benjamin's naming of Nietzsche is thus no less ambivalent than that analyzed by Nietzsche in the word *Schuld*. Nietzsche is addressed, as it were, *angesprochen* by Benjamin at the zenith of a certain *Verschuldung*, although it is not at all clear whether this *Verschuldung* is that of Nietzsche, as Benjamin suggests, or also and above all that of Benjamin himself, with respect to Nietzsche.[5]

To explore this ambiguity, let us reread the manner in which Benjamin mobilizes Nietzsche in the service of his argument (which is not, we recall, a demonstration). Following the assertion that God is not dead but has assumed a human destiny, Benjamin continues:

> This passage (*Durchgang*) of the planet man through the house of despair in the absolute solitude (*Einsamkeit*) of its course is the *ethos* defined by Nietzsche. This man is the overman, the first that, recognizing the capitalist religion, begins to fulfill it. Its fourth trait is that its God must be kept secret… ("Kapitalismus," 101/289)

The trait of modern man that Benjamin cites as defining the trajectory of "the planet man through the house of despair" – a trajectory that is deliberately couched in pagan, astrological terms[6] – is that of a certain *solitude, Einsamkeit*. Everything depends on just how this solitude is construed. By being associated here with the astrological movement of "the planet man through the house of despair," Benjamin emphasizes its *relationality*: this is not the isolated individual, but a being whose solitude is defined in terms of a complex constellation that is neither purely natural (i.e. astronomical), nor purely human. Least of all is it defined as "bare life," although it is determined by a "despair" that results from the "fall" of "transcendence." Benjamin's fascination with astrology, patent here, has at least two dimensions. First, it involves a relation to a cosmos that is neither immanently meaningful nor divinely symbolic: a move away from the religions of the Book, be they Christian or Judaic. Second, nature appears as a textual network to be read rather than as an image to be seen. This is why astrology and allegory are generally linked in his writing.

In "falling" then, the transcendence of the divine does not simply disappear: it lands squarely in the "destiny" of the "human": that is, in the net of guilt, whose strands are held together by the sentence of death as penalty and punishment. The problem, for Benjamin, is the way in which Nietzsche responds to the "fall":

> The thought of the *Übermensch* transposes the apocalyptic "leap" (*Sprung*) not into overturning (*Umkehr*), atonement (*Sühne*), purification, penance (*Büsse*), but rather into the ostensibly continuous, although ultimately explosive, discontinuous elevation (*Steigerung*). . . . The *Übermensch* is the historical man who has arrived at the sky and outgrown heaven without *turning around* (*ohne Umkehr*). ("Kapitalismus," 101/289)

Here, as always with Benjamin, but perhaps even more than usual, we have to be attentive to details. Note first, that the "fall" of transcendence – "God's transcendence has fallen" – has now become an "apocalyptic *leap*" – a *Sprung*. Benjamin does not take issue with this shift or translation, nor with its "apocalyptic" character. What he criticizes is that for Nietzsche this "leap" retains the character of the *leaper*, God, without subjecting it to a radical "turn-about," an *Umkehr*, a word that immediately recalls Hölderlin. The words that follow, however, are far more orthodox and Christian: atonement, purification, penance (*Sühne, Reinigung, Büsse*). Thus, while Benjamin is ostensibly reproaching Nietzsche – as Heidegger will do in his lectures of the 1930s – for remaining within the parameters of traditional Christian humanism and its conception of history, the language he uses is far closer to this conception than that of Nietzsche. At the same time, while criticizing it, Benjamin attributes a quality to Nietzsche's "ethos" that he himself will increasingly endorse in the years to come, namely, that of being "explosive" (*sprengend*):

> This explosion of the heavens (*Die Sprengung des Himmels*) through heightened humanity, which, religiously (even for Nietzsche) is and remains culpabilization-indebtedness (*Verschuldung*), was pre-judged (*präjudiziert*) by Nietzsche. And similarly by Marx: capitalism that does not overturn itself becomes, with simple and compound interest (*mit Zins und Zinseszins*), which are functions of *Schuld* (see the demonic ambiguity of this concept), socialism. ("Kapitalismus," 101–2/289)

Benjamin's move here, in thus targeting Nietzsche, is no less "ambiguous" than that he attributes to the word *Schuld*. For it was no one other than Nietzsche, of course, who extensively discussed this ambiguity and its implications in the second book of the *Genealogy of Morals*. Benjamin seems obliged to forget or to ignore this fact, and with it his own indebtedness toward Nietzsche, in order to take full credit for the argument expounded in *Capitalism as Religion*, which depends entirely on this ambiguity.

It is only by thus targeting Nietzsche, flanked and framed by Marx and Freud, that Benjamin is able to give his argument the semblance of a conclusion, by asserting not just that capitalism (and socialism as well) are religions, but more distinctively, that they are parasitic offshoots of Christianity:

> Capitalism developed itself – as could be shown not just with Calvinism, but with the other orthodox Christian tendencies – parasitically from Christianity in the west, so that *in the end* (*zuletzt*) its history is essentially that of a parasite, that of capitalism... The Christianity of the Reformation period did not simply favor the emergence of capitalism – it transformed itself into capitalism. ("Kapitalismus," 102/289)

Capitalism thus emerges here not just as a religion, but as the parasitic by-product of a particular religion, Christianity, which in taking over the host, takes control over Western history as well. In what way is the religion

of capitalism the parasite of Christianity? Precisely by exploiting the
"demonic ambiguity" of its culpabilizing *and* indebting power. How does it
accomplish this? Although Benjamin's text begins to dissolve at this point
into bibliographical notes, significantly right after targeting Nietzsche, Marx,
and Freud, it still manages to provide several hints of a possible response
to this question. Here is the first, jotted down in a kind of telegraphic
shorthand:

> Comparison between the images of saints of different religions on the one hand,
> and the banknotes of different states on the other. The Spirit that speaks out of
> the ornamentality (*Ornamentik*) of banknotes. ("Kapitalismus," 102/290)

The "spirit that speaks out of the *ornamentality* of banknotes" is not the
same spirit that speaks through the depictions of saints. But it is spirit
nevertheless. The spirit of capitalism. however, in contrast to the spirit of
Christianity, does not take as its point of departure depiction at all, for
instance that of the human body martyred and/or transfigured in faces
of suffering and hope. Rather, Benjamin contrasts such holy pictures with
the baroque ornamentation on banknotes. What previously would have
supplied a framework for a manifestation, now takes on its own value as
frame while at the same time separating itself from any possible "content."
For what it "signifies" is not individual suffering and the promise of its
transcendence, but the numeric measure of value as a social relation of force.
At the same time, however, Ornamentality is appropriate to a manifestation
that is fully cut off from that which it manifests, value, while at the same
time fulfilling the indispensable function of differentiating, measuring and
manifesting that value. But the "good news" that such banknotes bring
with them is that of their own capacity to circulate and be exchanged.
To that circulation and exchange they brook no alternative and it is this
exclusivity that provokes "cares: a spiritual malady that is peculiar to the
capitalist period" ("Kapitalismus," 102/290). Cares, of course, are what
call for religions in the first place, and as such are not limited to capitalism.
The particular bond that links cares to capitalism is that of *debt-as-guilt*, the
sense of being the author and owner of one's cares and torments: cares as
the private property of those they concern. This sense of proprietorship,

and hence of debt-as-guilt, is reinforced by the immanence and lack of alternative that distinguishes the world of capitalism.

> Spiritual (not material) impasse (*Ausweglosigkeit*) [leads to] poverty, vagrant, beggarly monasticism. A situation so devoid of any way out produces guilt and debt (*ist verschuldend*). ("Kapitalismus," 102/290)

In short, the religion of Capitalism, like the religions that preceded it: above all, Christianity, but also what Benjamin often refers to as a mythical (i.e. polytheistic) Paganism that he conceives as its predecessor, promotes *debt-as-guilt* as the *officially sanctioned response* to distress. This promotion of debt-as-guilt in turn reproduces and strengthens the sense of distress: "Cares are the index of the guilty consciousness of the impasse (*Ausweglosigkeit*)" and thus aid the "cult" to cultivate itself, without "truce or grace." But at the same time that care and guilt confirm that there is no way out (of the cult), they offer the only way "in": into the community. "Cares result from the anxiety of a communal, not an individual-material impasse." Cares, concerns, troubles and above all, the sense of debt-as-guilt hold together this new community, this church without dogma but also without end or limit. And yet, how is such an incessant und unlimited cult to be construed? It seems to have something to do with the ornaments on banknotes, with that in money that distinguishes it, as a sign of value, without representing that value in the way the sacred pictures of saints sought to represent the relation of suffering to beatitude. Such iconography has been supplanted by a certain ornamentality in capitalism, but this still does not tell us just how or why the latter should be considered the "parasite" of the former. The problem is even more complex in view of the fact that the distinctive quality of the capitalist religious cult, its permanence, stands in contrast if not contradiction to the necessity of a cult to be celebrated at specific times and places, and thus, not to be perennial and ongoing but rather discreet, limited, localizable and repeatable. How could a cult be both at the same time: localizable and ubiquitous, incessant and yet also clearly delimited and defined?

It is not in the fragmentary jottings of 1921 that elements of an answer to this question are to be found, but rather in other fragments, written some fifteen years later, and now collected in the volume on the "Paris Passages." I am thinking in particular of the notebook "B," dealing with "Fashion." For although he no longer refers directly to the earlier fragment, Benjamin's notes on *Mode* provide us with at least a partial instantiation of the cult he had announced but could not demonstrate in the text of 1921. In between the two writings he had articulated a notion that would enable him to negotiate the contradictions of capitalism as religion and as cult of *Verschuldung:* the notion of "allegory" elaborated in his study of 1924, *Origin of the German Mourning Play.* Allegory both intensifies and undermines the function of guilt: *intensifies,* insofar as it responds to a situation in which the possibility of redemption and grace being no longer a given, care and anxiety are all the greater and thus, the need for "guilt" all the stronger; *undermines,* however, insofar as there is no clear-cut authority or standard by which "guilt" could be determined.

Much of this ambivalence can be felt in Benjamin's discussions of fashion. The two mottoes he places at the head of his considerations sum up the two poles of the ambivalence. First, Leopardi: "Fashion: Lord Death, Lord Death!" Then, Balzac: "Rien ne meurt, tout se transforme": Nothing dies, everything changes.[7] Benjamin cites the phrase from Leopardi's "Dialogue of Fashion with Death" to suggest how fashion establishes a link between the religions of the past, in particular, Christianity, and the new religion of Capitalism. Benjamin adds a new scene to the encounter of fashion and death, which in his version is less of a dialogue and more of a pantomime:[7]

> Here fashion has introduced the dialectical turning-point (*Umschlageplatz*) between the female and the commodity – between lust and the corpse. Her tall and crude assistant (*flegelhafter Kommis*), death, measures the century with a yardstick, serves as model himself to save money and organizes single-handedly the liquidation, the fire-sale that in French is called "revolution." For fashion was never anything else but the parody of the colorful corpse, provocation of death through the female, and between shrill laughter learned by rote, the bitterly whispered dialogue with decay. That is fashion. Therefore it changes so rapidly; tickles death and is already someone else again, someone new, when he finally turns around to strike her. For a hundred years she owed him nothing (*ist ihm … nichts schuldig geblieben*). Now finally she is about to abandon the field to him. He however, on the banks of a new Lethe that carries the asphalt stream

through passages – he donates (*stiftet*) the armature of the whore as a trophy. Revolution. Love. (*Passagen-Werk* III/62–3)

Fashion, for Benjamin, defines itself through its parodic if also bitter dialogue with death, which is also one with decay. Death and fashion are joined together by their shared interest in the human body and its relation to time. Time, the medium of change, can be that of constant renewal or steady decline. With the Reformation, the pendulum inclined toward the latter rather than the former, at least from the perspective of Benjamin's *Origin of the German Mourning Play*. Mourning the loss of a transparent relation to transcendence, *Trauer*, Benjamin writes, "reanimates with masks (*maskenhaft neubelebt*) the emptied world" (1978: 318), a world in which action and "good works" are no longer the guarantee of grace. Out of this theatrical turn of mourning toward the *mask* in order to produce at least the semblance of a reanimation that according to Luther otherwise had become accessible to "faith alone" – out of this theatrical turn of the Baroque emerges "fashion," which seeks to outwit death at its own game: that of mastering time. Time itself has shifted from serving as a *narrative* medium – medium of Christian soteriology – to becoming a *theatrical* one: that of the *Trauerspiel*, in the German Baroque, but also that of fashion in nineteenth-century Paris. This shift in the medial function of time also entails a certain spatialization: that of the stage, the scene, and the theater. The absence of what Benjamin, using a term borrowed from Erich Unger, often refers to as the "force of the frame" (*Gewalt des Rahmens*[8]), ushers in the necessity of an audience, spectators, addressees, in order to take the place of an authority that is no longer authorized. With the weakening of the Christian narrative that hitherto comprehended and contained the passage of time, this passage must be dealt with otherwise, and it is here that fashion – and death – intervene. Death thus assists fashion in the effort to cover up, if not overcome, the disastrous effects of time. But the spread of commodity-production and consumption assigns a new role to death by placing it at the center of a system of production based upon the consumption of the producers. Already in the seventeenth century, Benjamin argued, this altered sense of time and history placed death, and the corpse, at the center of its preoccupations: "From the viewpoint of death, life is the production of corpses" (*GS* I, 392) and corpses, in turn, the epitome and paradigm of the "allegorizing of the phusis" (391). Fashion continues this allegorizing in the nineteenth (and following) centuries and at the same time ritualizes it. The predominance of the commodity, which Benjamin investigates throughout the *Passages*, provides fashion with both its condition of possibility and its components. Condition of possibility, in investing things both with new life-like allegories, commodities signify independently of what appears to be their spontaneous, inherent existence. And components, since the elements of fashion consist of the body exposed to time, coupled with the concealment of its most devastating effects. Each time death looks around in order to "strike" (*um sie zu schlagen*), fashion is already elsewhere, having changed its guise and its place in order to implement the motto of Balzac, "Nothing dies, everything changes." At the same time – and it really is at the same time – nothing dies, because everything, qua commodity, is already dying, which is to say, taking leave of itself, insofar as "self" names the unity of that which stays the same over time. And yet, paradoxically, fashion underscores the paradox that everything stays the same even while searching to be new and different. But the sameness of fashion is precisely a *sameness without self*.[9]

It is this that perhaps explains the place that replaces the field of battle that Fashion has now abandoned: "the banks of a new Lethe," that "rolls through the passages in the stream of asphalt." The *Passages* are organized to encourage both the forgetting of death and its commemoration. Both converge in the commodity as an object of desire, especially when that commodity is inseparable from a human body: that of the whore. But it is not the whore as such, her face or her body, that death "donates" as "trophy" marking the defeat, or at least the retreat, of Fashion: it is "the armature" (*die Armature*), a word that returns frequently in Benjamin's writings on the passages, and that points toward the hidden framework that allows things to be seen, displayed, exhibited, desired, purchased, and consumed – but which itself remains generally unnoticed. One could say that one of the primary tendencies of Benjamin's work on the *Passages* is to call attention to the invisible *armature*, its necessity and its ramifications.

The word is, like so many others, itself a network of significations. Coming from "arms," it suggests shields and struggles, defense and assault, but also bodily members, although not necessarily human ones. In this particular case, the "armature" also names the frame of the brassiere and of clothing generally, the hidden construct that gives form to that which conceals in exhibiting and exhibits in concealing: in short, the ideal object of desire. The armature both delimits bodies, desire, and commodities, and at the same time allows them to circulate. On the banks of the new Lethe, the *Passages*, it becomes a "trophy" commemorating a previous victory while also facilitating the desire to forget the "Lord" or "Mistress" who now commands the scene: "Herr" or "Madama Morte."

Fashion is back in fashion, today, almost a century after Benjamin wrote that it combined a sense of "coming things" with an aversion to the immediate past. At a time when one of the most popular slogans, in politics as in business, is the exhortation to "move forward," and to do so without looking back, Benjamin's observation is more suggestive than ever:

> A definitive perspective on fashion emerges only from the observation that to each generation the one that has just flowed past (*die gerade verflossene*) appears as the most thorough-going anti-aphrodisiac. (B 1a/4)

> A thoroughly related problem emerged concerning the new velocities, which brought a changed rhythm into life. This too was at first tried out playfully. Roller coasters appeared and the Parisians adopted this entertainment as though obsessed... Fashion provided satisfaction since the beginning for this enigmatic need for the sensational. Only a theological approach, however, can get to the bottom of this need, since out of it speaks a profound, affective human attitude toward the course of history. (B 2/1)

The drive to "move forward" is of course, as Nietzsche again had analyzed, always also and perhaps above all the drive to move away from the past — from a past that is at the same time a harbinger of the future. Speed only accelerates this process, with all of its ambivalence. Fashion participates in this acceleration, in this move forward and away from the past while at the same time staying the same, and in so doing, it offers a sort of consolation and hope to a self that also hopes to stay the same, to survive as self-same. But instead of the self, what is left is the armature as a *sameness without self.* Which is not to say that the self disappears. On the contrary, it remains the motor of a more general acceleration of traffic, the tempo with which information is transmitted, with which newspaper editions relay and relieve one another (*sich ablösen*) – this all amounts to the attempt to eliminate all breaking off (*alles Abbrechen*), all rough ends and abrupt endings (*jähe Enden*) and [the insight into] how death as interruption (*Einschnitt*) hangs together with all the straight lines of the divine course of time (*mit allen Geraden des göttlichen Zeitverlaufes zusammenhängt*). (B 2/4)

What Benjamin describes, however, is not quite what he asserts, as developments since he wrote this have made abundantly clear. What he describes is not simply the "elimination" of "all breaking off" – *alles Abbrechen* – through the rapid succession of information, but rather the integration of the *break* into the "news" – as "breaking news," which fills in the gaps between the true "breaks," which of course are commercial: "Stay with us, we'll be right back after a short break." After the break – back to breaking news, designed, as with fashion, to break, but also channel, the forward rush of time toward a more definitive break that challenges the staying – power of the "self." Fashion, and the "news," which has adopted its rhythm, can be said to "mimic" and "parody" death insofar as they stage the break with the aim of covering it over, as it covers, and exposes, the bodies of its "models." These bodies are exhibited as "models" in that they seem to have already absorbed and survived the break, rendering it survivable to the spectator.

The same could be said of the "ending," which remains "abrupt," but which the acceleration of tempo strives to integrate into a spectacle that can be seen in its entirety and thus survived. "Abruptness" frames this sight according to a principle that Benjamin, writing on epic theater, was one of the first to formulate: that of the formative power of *interruption*.[10] The "abruptness of endings" is thus integrated as interruption into a network – which is to say, into a net of relations that only works, only becomes a *work*, insofar as its mortal openness is framed, formed and rendered meaningful by a *linear narrative* that Benjamin does not hesitate to designate as *divine* (*göttlich*). Such a narrative is implied in his surmise that "death as interruption (*Einschnitt*) hangs together with all the straight-lines of the divine course of time (*Zeitverlaufes*)." (B 2/4)

Such "hanging together," however – which ties dispersed strands together and makes of them a network – always presupposes the exercise of a certain legitimating force, if not violence: a *Gewalt*. Benjamin, who shortly after this passage writes of the "force of fashion (*Gewalt der Mode*) over the city of Paris," concludes his observations on the interruptive force of fashion with the following questions: "Were there fashions in Antiquity? Or were they prohibited by the 'force of the frame' (*Gewalt des Rahmens*)?" (B 2/4). The second question suggests that where the frame has sufficient force to enforce closure, there is neither room nor need for fashion. The necessity of the latter, consequently, arises only where the "force of the frame" is too weak to impose its authority. Where the frame has gone underground, as it were, and become an *armature*. This is the situation in which fashion emerges to take the place and assume the function of a linear eschatological narrative by giving meaning to interruption and to abrupt endings. With fashion, the armature is what transforms the net into a network.

All of this is itself hidden away in the banality of a word that is difficult to translate into English. It occurs in a passage that describes the speed with which information is transmitted, in particular by "newspaper editions [that] *replace and relay* one another." The German word, that I translate here, inadequately, as "replace and relay," is: *sich ablösen*. The root of the verb, *ablösen*, is cognate with the English "loose" or "loosen" and designates the *loosening of bonds or ties*. Acceleration, epitomized in fashion but by no means limited to it, diminishes the significance of the single, isolated self-contained place, held together by its armature, by increasing the power of moving from place to place, thereby decreasing the time required to traverse distance. The goal of acceleration is thus that of being able to be here and elsewhere at one and the same time. The time of this simultaneity has to be "one and the same" if that which takes place in it is to be considered *similar*, indeed, *identical to itself*. By thus reducing the time of traversal, the self seeks absolute mobility while remaining itself: hence, the worship of everything that is or appears to be "auto-mobile," including the speed with which information is processed and circulates. The cult of speed is thus a cult of power: that of appropriating time and space for a Self that thereby hopes to extricate itself from the heterogeneous *net* of relations by transforming it into a *network*, whether of automobiles, computers, persons or things. Such a project however also implies that individuals cease operating as static, isolated and self-contained elements and instead begin to function as *components*, always in the process of being relieved and replaced (*abgelöst*), extricated from fixed positions in the net in order to circulate in the network. Acceleration, by seeking to eliminate or integrate all "breaks and abrupt endings," thus entails a *consecration* of time, since "death as interruption hangs together with all the straight lines of the divine course of time." Acceleration and its interruption – whether in fashion, production or circulation – are what results when the "straightaway of the divine course of time" extends and descends to earth as the hidden deity of the capitalist cult.

If acceleration thus entails a certain process of dissolution, of *lösen*, this word suggests another connection (*Zusammenhang*) between death and the divine described in the penultimate paragraph of "Capitalism as Religion":

> Connection (*Zusammenhang*) between the dogma of the dissolving (*auflösenden*) – for us in this capacity at the same time redeeming and killing (*erlösenden und tötenden*) – nature of knowledge with capitalism: the bottom-line (*die Bilanz*) as redeeming and disposing (*erlösende und erledigende*) knowledge. (103/290)

The "straightaway of the divine course of history" that is presupposed by the experience of death as interruption, as *Einschnitt*, has come down to earth in and as the *bottom-line* of capitalist double bookkeeping. If Benjamin had begun by asserting that "capitalism is a religion consisting of mere cult, without dogma," (102/290), then we see here that the "without" in this affirmation does not maintain itself as simple exclusion. It marks a connection, a *Zusammenhang*: the cult of capitalism may be *without* dogma, but as such it still stands *in relation to* dogma. Not however to the manifest dogma of revealed religion, but to a dogma that is as hidden as the god it worships. Death as interruption, as final cut (*Einschnitt*), joins with the infinite straightaway it negates to produce the discrete but incessant bottom-line of profit and loss. This bottom-line "dissolves" everything leading up, or down, to it, in producing a final result that ostensibly offers a ground upon which one can stand, upon which one can ostensibly *count*.

But the result of this accounting – a certain conception of "knowledge" – "solves" the problem only by dissolving it: it "redeems" (*erlöst*) from debt-as-guilt only by "killing" (*tötend*). Such knowledge as bottom-line absolves the "living" from "destiny" only by putting an end to their lives, inscribing their lives in an actuarial table that would frame all that has been and will be. In this sense, it is not just the past that is "absolved" but also the future: or at least, this is the dogma of the bottom-line that is hidden behind the "fearful pomp" of a cult ostensibly without dogma. Instead, there is the cult of knowledge as information whose circulation is no longer separable from the cult itself. Knowledge as information is its medium. This knowledge as information follows the binary logic of the capitalist balance-sheet, with truth and untruth, good and evil modeled after profit and loss. Just as the bottom-line marks the caesura of that which alone is held to *count*, so the dogma of knowledge aims at producing a result that can absolve itself of all that has come before and that will come after. Knowledge becomes dogmatic when it is absolved of all relation and liberated, redeemed, detached – *erlöst* – from all *obligations* to past and future. Past and future themselves are absorbed and forgotten in the eternal presence of a bottom-line that is no longer static, no longer stays put, but *moves forward*, annexing the future to the present and thus mimicking eternal life.

As a dynamic, progressive network, knowledge is designed to accomplish the work of redeeming from debt-as-guilt by absolving, dissolving and resolving it into a profitable bottom-line. But in so doing, it is also death-bringing, *tötend*, in its search to impose an end that would be ultimate and definitive. This struggle to impose an end is however itself endless, giving rise to a "universal" and unending "polemic," just as the cult it celebrates strives to be "permanent."

It is also all-inclusive. In the final paragraph of his text, Benjamin suggests that much could be learned about capitalism as a religion by recalling how an "original paganism" did not construe of religion as something "higher" or "moral," but rather as something "immediately practical"; and that in so doing, it was no more clear on its "ideal" or "transcendent" nature than capitalism is today.

Rather it saw in the individual of its community who was irreligious or of another faith precisely for that reason a full-fledged member, as today's bourgeoisie sees in those of its members who are not gainfully employed (*in seinen nicht erwerbenden Angehörigen*). ("Kapitalismus," 103/291)

If capitalism is a religion that recognizes and accepts as its own even those who do not share its "faith" or who "are not gainfully employed," it is because its cult requires neither faith nor gainful employment (*Erwerb*). All it requires is the "bare life" of the living, to be sustained. Or rather, what it requires is the consciousness of self as bare life. And as bottom-line. For the bottom-line is what remains of the fallen transcendence, of a God who has assumed the human destiny of debt-as-guilt, and who therefore has gone into hiding. This God can be addressed only "at the zenith of his indebtedness," a zenith that appears, paradoxically, only as the letterhead at the top of the balance sheet: unripe because never definitive, always only a stage in the ongoing descent toward the bottom-line. It is this descent that describes the trajectory of the cult "sans trêve et sans merci."

The divine straight-away thus cut off by the bottom line could thus be seen as a development of precisely the dilemma announced by Benjamin at the outset of this text, which he did not publish and which he suggested could never really be written:

> We cannot draw closed the net in which we stand. Later however there will be an overview. (100/288)

What can be "looked over," surveyed: *überblickt*, is the balance-sheet. In it, the net comes together into a network, with a bottom-line exercising the "force of the frame." To draw up the net in which one stands, however, is hardly an image of emancipation from debt-as-guilt, but rather its perpetuation: a perpetuation rife with "universal polemics." But from where, then, is this overview possible: where does it take its stand? And in so targeting the bottom-line, does it *overlook* the net?

A hint of an answer can perhaps be found in a text written by Benjamin some seven years earlier, a text he called "his first major work": a reading of two poems of Hölderlin, "*Dichtermut*" (Poet's Courage) and "*Blödigkeit*" ("Timidity"). Benjamin wrote this essay in 1914 under the impact of the death of his friend, the poet, Fritz Heinle. Not surprising, therefore, that the central problem around which Benjamin's reading turns involves the relation of the poet to death, and through this, that of "the living," *des Lebendigen*, a Hölderlinian turn of phrase, to the *Divine*. It is Benjamin's interpretation of this term, which he takes over from Hölderlin and which is the marker of an enormous debt, that is of particular interest in the context of our previous discussion. For as we have seen, the notion of the *Lebendigen* is, implicitly at least, at the hidden heart of "Capitalism as Religion," insofar as the cult that defines this religion is based on *Schuld*: debt-as-guilt, which in turn is inseparable from the *living, den Lebendigen*. Inseparable, but not univocal, and Benjamin's reading of Hölderlin opens a *space* in which an alternative notion of *Schuld*, and of its relation to nets and networks, begins to emerge. And the space opened by Benjamin in this text relates to his surprising interpretation of the "living" in Hölderlin's "world" precisely *as a certain kind of space*, or rather, as a kind of *stretching*:

> The living are always clearly, in this world of Hölderlin, the *stretching (Erstreckung)* of space, the map or surface (*Plan*) spread out, within which, (as will become visible) destiny stretches (*sich das Schicksal erstreckt*)... Much, much more about Hölderlin's cosmos is said in the following words, which – alien as though from an Eastern world and nevertheless how much more original than the Greek Parca – confer majesty upon the poet. "Does not your foot tread upon truth, as upon carpets?" ("*Geht auf Wahrem dein Fuß nicht, wie auf Teppichen?*")

It is no doubt quite a "stretch" from this gloss on "the living" to the debt-and-guilt-ridden cult of capitalism-as much as between the "carpets" on which the poet's foot *treads* to the "net in which we *stand*." And yet in the very extremities of this stretch can be read the outlines of a medium through which an alternative to the cult of capitalism becomes thinkable. The determination of "the living" as *Erstreckung* appeals to a notion of space that is quite different from the traditional conception of extension (which is how it is translated in the English edition). Rather, *Erstreckung*, a favorite word of Benjamin, is one he will later use to describe Brecht's epic theater, where it is designed, he writes, to "expunge all traces of the sensational."[11] *Sensation*, a notion he also develops with respect to the speed of the capitalist cults of fashion and information, involves the lust for "breaking news" in order to break up the lethal monotony of the self-same. "Stretching," by contrast, carries something other, although not necessarily new, into the space of the living, or rather into the living room as *Raum*. The German word, *Raum*, which is generally translated as space, would be better translated as "room," with which it is cognate. *Raum*, in contrast to "space," can imply delimitation, as it does when Benjamin uses it to define "the living." It is not just space as abstract extension, but a very distinctive form of "stretching" related to situated bodies: to "stretch" is to presuppose a predetermined "room" rather than an indeterminate "space." Benjamin's effort therefore is always directed toward exploring the nature of this "room" and what happens when it begins to "stretch." This is why the figure of the *carpet* is so important: it is that to which "the true," upon which the poet *treads*, is likened. What interests Benjamin most of all in this Hölderlinian carpet is its *Musterhaftigkeit*, that is, its *patterning*. This patterning is also exemplary, since, as the English translator notes, the German word, *musterhaft*, can mean both exemplary and patterning. Unfortunately, in retaining *only* "exemplary" in the body of the translation, the translator makes the wrong choice, since precisely what is exemplary about the *Muster* is its *patterning*, not its specific *content*. The truth upon which the poet *proceeds* are *carpets*, in the plural, whose singular magic resides in their distinctive patterning. Benjamin makes this unmistakable clear when he interprets the patterning as "ornament":

> Just as in the image of the carpet (posited as a level for an entire system) what must be remembered is its *Musterhaftigkeit*, its patterning, the spiritual arbitrariness (*geistige Willkür*) of the ornament – and ornament therefore constitutes a true determination of layout (*Lage*), rendering it *absolute* – there thus resides within the traversable (*beschreitbar*) order of truth itself the intensive activity of the gait (*des Ganges*) as inner, plastic, temporal form. (115/27)

This emphasis on ornamental patterning as that which makes layout absolute anticipates Benjamin's remark on the "ornamentality" of the effigies on banknotes that replaces the iconography of sacred figures in traditional (above all, Christian) religion. However, whereas the iconic figurality of revealed religion is inscribed within, and framed by an eschatological and soteriological narrative – here, in Benjamin's reading of Hölderlin, time is taken up into the figure of the carpet as that upon which the poet must *tread*. *The poet treads, but does not stand.* And what he treads upon is not a stable place but a *stretched layout*, one which by any stretch of the imagination is difficult to conceive. This *Lage*, layout, is rendered "absolute" by the exemplariness of its patterning. The usual rendering of *Lage* in English as "situation" is misleading precisely insofar as the word here does *not* imply the self-contained stability of a *situs*, but rather the unstable dynamics of an ongoing relation. The *layout* is always temporally determined as that which has been *laid down, gelegen*:[12] "Room can be grasped as the identity of *Lage* and *Gelegenem*: of layout and laid-down." As with the carpet, such an "identity of layout and laid-down" invites and indeed enjoins a traversal: it must be *tread upon* without there ever being an assured exit or ending:

> This region of the spirit is traversable (*beschreitbar*) and necessarily leaves those who traverse it (*den Schreitenden*) with each arbitrary step (*Willkürschritte*) in the realm of the true. (115/27)

In other words, "the temporal existence" of the Living is caught up in an "infinite stretching," with respect to which "identity" can be defined as the coincidence of the layout with the laid-down, the *Lage* with the *Gelegenen*. What is "laid down" – *gelegen* – however can never be predicted. And it is here that the admonition of Hölderlin's poem assumes its full force: "Was geschieht, es sei alles gelegen dir!" (Whatever happens let it all be laid down for you). "Laid down for you" – *dir gelegen* – should not be read as suggesting that everything has been intended or designed with the poet in mind, but rather something quite different: that the poet, and with him the Living, remain true to what has been laid down as their layout, which means true to a stretching of space by time that supports a movement, a treading going nowhere, except perhaps toward a *sameness without self*. This formula, which is not to be found in Benjamin, to be sure, nevertheless perhaps begins to approximate what in this essay he designates as a "relation" that would be "*of* Genius" but not "*to* it." This "*Gelegenheit*" or *opportunity* to which the genius of the poet *responds*, is not one, however, that can be *targeted*, for a layout can never be put in its place, least of all through the virtuality of a figure (*Gestalt*). The layout that has been laid-down cannot be put in its place because its "identity" consists in the stretching of place itself, the *Erstreckung des Raumes*. Nothing can simply be put in its place when the place itself is being stretched and laid-out – nothing except what Benjamin here calls "imagistic dissonance" (*Bilddissonanz*), which, like that of rhyme, which it echoes, involves sameness without self, repetition without equality. In this sense, opportunity, "Gelegenheit," can be said to signify "the spiritual-temporal identity (the truth) of the layout." (117/29) It is an event and as such cannot be made an object of cognition or appropriation. It is the event of a net-without-work: a *netting* without net profit or loss.

A serious reading of this essay would have to explore and elaborate the ways in which the "dissonance of the image" does not simply abolish targeting and figuration, to be sure, but alters their *course:* "Precisely after all the extremes of imagery (*Bildhaftigkeit*), a path and apt goal (*schickliches Ziel*) must be visible differently now..." (117/29). Benjamin will go on to describe this difference in terms of "a peculiar doubling of the figure" in the second poem studied in the essay, "Timidity." But for the purposes of the present discussion, it will be sufficient to recall the manner in which his reading draws to a close, draws a bottom-line but without drawing up the net in which it stands, and indeed by suggesting the inappropriateness of any definitive conclusion:

> In the end it cannot be a matter of the investigation of ultimate elements, for the last word of this world is just that of solidarity and obligation, of *Verbundenheit:* as the unity of the function of binding and bound. (122/32)

The term, *Verbundenheit*, is much stronger than the English "connection," used in the published translation, would suggest. To be *verbunden* is not merely to be *connected*, but to be *bound up with, obliged, bonded*, and therefore not always separable from a certain *bondage*. It does not *extricate* the Living from the net in which they stand, but rather redefines *Schuld* as an effect not of *standing* but of *going: treading* on and in an irreducible net of *relations* that defines the room not only of poetry but of all *patterning*, and defines it as something to which one must respond: as Benjamin in this essay responds to what he calls the *Gedichtete*, the "poeticized," but also, more etymologically, the "dictated." To affirm such *Verbundenheit* is to acknowledge the obligation to respond, not just to persons, things or subjects, but to the "sole rule of relation" that for Benjamin is the "principle of the poeticized."

The adjectival noun, *das Gedichtete*, suggests that the net of relations that constitute it should not be confused with a work, an accomplished and meaningful whole. To be sure, there will always be, always have been, targeting, and the *net* will always have been made to *work*. But the affirmation of *Verbundenheit* makes its way on a carpet whose exemplary pattern will never be reducible to a bottom-line, any more than its opportunity to a target. For what is laid down opportunely (*gelegen*) will always be just another knot or node in the net.

NOTES

1. "In capitalism, things have a meaning only in their relationship to the cult." "Capitalism as Religion," 288.
2. This holds for the somewhat earlier text on "Language in general...," in which language is defined in terms of its "immediate" or "unmediated" impartibility" (*unmittelbare Mitteilbarkeit*).
3. Although *Le Crépuscule du soir* had appeared in the original 1857 edition of *Les Fleurs du mal*, it became part of the *Tableaux Parisiens* section of the revised 1861 edition. The text of both editions can be found at http://www.fleursdumal.org/.
4. The expression is used in precisely this way by another author that Benjamin would later, in his notebooks, cite occasionally, Paul Lafargue, who in the introduction to *Le droit à la pareses*, written in 1983 while imprisoned, described the situation of the workers in these terms: "La morale capitaliste, piteuse parodie de la morale chrétienne, frappe d'anathème la chair du travailleur; elle prend pour idéal de réduire le producteur au plus petit minimum de besoins, de supprimer ses joies et ses passions et de le condamner au rôle de machine délivrant du travail sans trêve ni merci." An English translation of Lafargue's *The Right to be Lazy*, including its Preface, can be found at http://www.marxists.org/archive/lafargue/1883/lazy/index.htm.
5. Benjamin's ambivalence toward Nietzsche recalls in many respects that of Heidegger: both laud and also criticize Nietzsche for his articulations of a certain nihilism. Above all, they seek to put him in his (proper) place, in order thereby better to define their own.

6. Those who would believe that "pagan" (*heidnisch*) is for Benjamin simply a term of reproach or critique would do well to remember his avowed and constant fascination with astrology.

7. Benjamin's citation also changes the gender of death, which in Leopardi's dialogue is feminine: "Madama Morte" rather than "Herr Tod." In Leopardi's text, Fashion reminds Death that they are sisters: "Non ti ricordi che tutte e due siamo nate dalla Caducità?" (Leopardi, 1979: I.7).

8. See *Das Passagen-Werk*, GS VI, 115 (B 2, 4). *Ursprung des deutschen Trauerspiels*, p. 96.

9. This is also the formula that comes closest to designating the paradox of Nietzsche's "Eternal Return of the Same." Benjamin was fascinated with the notion of the Eternal Return, which however – once again targeting Nietzsche – he sought to reattribute to Blanqui's *Eternité par les astres*, written in prison at the end of his life.

10. "Interruption is one of the most fundamental procedures in producing form." Benjamin, *Was ist das epische Theater?* (2), GS II.2, 536. This is, of course, a modern version of the Aristotelian theory of *peripeteia* as an essential constituent of complex tragic plots.

11. Benjamin describes Brecht's theater, for instance, as an "*epische Erstreckung*" which he in turn compares to the action of the Ballet Master on his female pupils, stretching their limbs "to the limits of the possible." GS II. 2, p. 533. Applied not just to bodies but also to places, *Erstreckung* becomes the *Schwelle* (threshold, swelling) that characterizes the Paris of the Passages. Cf. among many other instances, C2, 3, C2 a 3.

12. *Gelegen* is the part participle of *liegen*, to lie (down). Benjamin, following Hölderlin, is contrasting two aspects of what in English might be designated as the "lay of the land." To emphasize the temporal aspect of the participle, I have translated *gelegen* not simply as "lay" but as "laid-down."

REFERENCES

Benjamin, Walter (1972–1989), "Kapitalismus als Religion," *Gesammelte Schriften* (*GS*), vol. 6, Suhrkamp Verlag: Frankfurt am Main, 100–3.

English: "Capitalism as Religion," *Selected Writings*, vol. I, eds Marcus Bullock and Michael W. Jennings. Cambridge, MA: Harvard UP, 1996, 288–91.

—— (1972–1989), "Schicksal und Charakter." *GS* II.1, 171–9. English: "Fate and Character," *Selected Writings*, vol. I, 201–6.

—— (1972–1989), "Was ist das epische Theater? (2)," *GS* II.2, 532–9. English: "What Is the Epic Theater? (II)," *Selected Writings*, vol. 4, eds Howard Eiland and Michael W. Jennings. Cambridge, MA: Harvard UP, 2003.

—— (1972–1989), "Zwei Gedichte von Friedrich Hölderlin," *GS* II.1, 105–26. English: "Two Poems of Friedrich Hölderlin," *Selected Writings*, vol. I, 18–36.

—— (1978), *Ursprung des deutschen Trauerspiels*. Suhrkamp: Frankfurt am Main. English: *Origin of the German Tragic Drama*, London/New York: Verso, 1985.

—— (1983), *Das Passagen-Werk*, 2 vols. Suhrkamp: Frankfurt am Main. English: *The Arcades Project*. Cambridge: Harvard UP, 1999.

Blanqui, Louis Auguste (1973), *Instructions pour une prise d'armes, L'éternité par les astres, hypothèse astronomique, et autres texts*, eds Miguel Abensour and Valentin Pelosse. Paris: Société encyclopédique française.

Lafargue, Paul (1965), *Le droit à la paresse*. Paris: F. Maspero.

Leopardi, Giacomo (1979), *Operette morali*. Milano: Fondazione Arnoldo e Alberto Mondadori.

Schreber, Daniel Paul (1903, Trans. & Rpt. 2000) *Denkwürdigkeiten eines Nervenkranken*. Leipzig: O. Mutze. English: *Memoirs of My Nervous Illness*. New York: New York Review of Books.

Steiner, Uwe (1998), "Kapitalismus als Religion: Anmerkungen zu einem Fragment Walter Benjamins," *Deutsche Vierteljahrsschrift für Literaturwissenschaft und Geistesgeschichte*, 72: 147–71.

Tübingen, J.C.B. Mohr. English: *The Protestant Ethic and the Spirit of Capitalism*. Trans. Talcott Parsons. New York: Scribner's.

Unger, Erich (1921; Republished 1989) *Politik und Metaphysik*. Wurzburg: Konigshausen & Neumann.

Weber, Max (1920, Trans. 1930) *Die protestantische Ethik und der "Geist" des Kapitalismus*. In Bd. I of *Gesammelte Aufsätze zur Religionssoziologie*.

CHAPTER 8

Disparity, Information, and Consumption – Hello to an Agonistics of the Future

Sande Cohen

The first few pages of this paper discuss information and consumption across scientific and aesthetic domains, emphasizing a related disturbance or disparity in these areas. I then discuss information and consumption as conceived by some of those French "theorists" of the 1960s to 1980s who elicited and added to the ambiguity of criticism, exploring some of their contestable notions about information and consumption. I conclude with a few ideas about criticism in an age of information/consumption upheavals and new/old cultural-political stabilities.

These days, consumption and information are contested concepts. What do they name and explain? I start with the assumption that from political-economy to cultural studies, traditional and newly reformatted, consumption and information evoke disturbance. Indeed, one author insists that in considering "abstract sex" or "virtual body-sex," received information and consumption organized by binaries (male/female), the metaphysics of "is" and "versus," is all but useless. In understanding a "reversibility" from new information and how we consume gender and power, we should start with:

> ...sex is an event: the actualization of modes of communication and reproduction of information that unleashes an indeterminate capacity to affect all levels of organization of a body ... an envelope that folds and unfolds the most indifferent elements, substances, forms and functions of connection and transmission. (Parisi, 2004: 13)

Information and consumption have brought us to the point where we can affirm "artifice has always been part of nature ... the unpredictable mutations of the body" (Parisi, 2004: 13). Here, information clearly changes consumption, with unknown reverberations. Yet what a demographer using these concepts gives to think is not necessarily congruent with what microscopic cultural analysis figures forth – through newspaper, television, radio, and Internet, *each* listener (consumer) receives from a *one-to-many* medium the "fact," itself a condensation of measuring and evaluating, that half the world's population lives on or consumes two dollars per day; a moment later comes the cultural information that the Walt Disney Music Hall in LA cost $US 275 million so as to merge contemporary music, cultural advertising, institutional vitality, and tourism. Is each consumed as "the price paid," two dollars a day to stand as an object of pity and 275 million an object of necessity? There is enough disturbance in *comparing* such information and its consumption to ask which is the complex number here? And to ask: how are micro- and macroscopic context(s) given such numbers?

As soon as one notes that information and consumption often do not "fit" with a static idea of context assigned to these concepts, we can connect with their disturbance. For instance, writers in the cross-discipline of "audit studies" have noted that the introduction of state-sponsored systematic auditing in English universities was at once to invoke a nearly unassailable spell, "audit" a "good," a taking of "responsibility," yet which also functions as a "political technology of the self," practices of auditing joined with "empowerment," "enabling," "self-management," professors becoming "service-providers" of information in ways of treating it and students "customers" (see Strathern, 2000: 289). Consumption and information are more than just fluid and relative, but also perplexing – because such stalwart procedures as the comparative method are also sources of problems. Student plus customer disturbs what? Does reflection become a disparity of consuming information, even in the remaining knowledge zones of the arts and humanities, once resources given to remediation use knowledge but generate only a practice?

In this paper, information and consumption are assumed to have been decontextualized or subject to decontextualization by the ongoing processes of producing new information set amidst changed forms of consumption, hence they are concepts, practices, and effects both structural and historical. Information and consumption are an opportunity to ask some questions.[1] Chief among them are: how are information and consumption stand-alone or even stand-together concepts and relations? What to do with notice of other, related, concepts: control, production, dissemination, differentiation, identity, simulation, new class distortions, as well as understanding the minute decisions people make and have to make? How could information and consumption be separate from destinies and outcomes, including those concerning the consequences of basic social practices – doesn't every book and work of art offer a share of Enlightenment? This is certainly not as straightforward as Manuel Castells has it, who says that information issues congeal into an "I think, therefore I produce," whose operative terms are "rich" and "poor," modeled on "outputs" from national economies. Does the idealization of "smart-work" model anything other than itself, and is "smart-work" the same in product design, in teaching K-1, in scholarly criticism? What do authors such as Castells actually mean when they insist that an information-driven society pivots on the capacity of knowledge acting on knowledge? When was that not the case, since the history of ancient Greece shows clearly that semiotics and autopsy were closely linked as signs and outcomes (Castells quoted in McSherry, 2001: 5). Just because we see an intensification where US universities are more proactive in securing their "relevance" to their consumers, it is not clear that relevance and service are intrinsic to intellectual autonomy, academic freedom, the public domain and private interests that line up with only "rich" and "poor" (McSherry, 2001: 37).

There are many angles of contention. Are information and consumption part of a new Foucauldian type episteme, these days discussed as a society of "risk," one that accelerates, among other feelings and conditions, persistent fear of obsolescence in all spheres of life, exactly as society seems to welcome more social heterogeneity, banishing sexism and racism from public expression as new organizations of racism and sexism become more entangled? Or should we think of risk as symmetrical, as Stephen Pinker does: "The contradiction of courtship – flaunt your desire while playing hard to get – comes from two parts of romantic love: setting a minimum standard for candidates in the mate market, and capriciously committing body and soul to one of them" (1997: 419)? That's amusing, but also glib. The globalization of intellectual labor, as Dion Dennis points out, means that American higher-education turns what are social risks – how to, say, make medical knowledge available or add to contemporary debates about slavery reparations – into private embodiment before returning to the public. Knowledge means one has to be informed as to which college degree adds to "lifetime income enhancement." The academic degree is a consumer item in a new political economy where the holder of the degree assumes risk for its usefulness. Tell me your assessment of risk and I'll tell you who you are becoming (Dennis, 2003). What is entailed by calling ourselves "informed" if to be so mostly comes to describing what one *performs* – illocutes – as certain functions within the division of labor? If it is a question that information and consumption do belong to a new episteme, a rupture with prior forms of organization, should we continue to talk about information and consumption as inherently connected with anti-information (lies) and anti-consumption (inoperable objects), with non-information (redundancy absorbs content) and non-consumption (pleasure), with a-information (ambiguity) and a-consumption (action without goal), with all the other concepts, evocations, and relations that indicate simultaneous action and assemblage of these concepts/relations?

Information and consumption *are* agonistics. As concepts and historical entities, they remain threaded to what Gerard Genette has called a methodological "betrayal" – information and consumption are not natural objects or relations and so discussion of them should abandon any mimesis about them. Their likeness has to be theorized (see the comments of Genette, 1995: 331ff.). Information and consumption might be deployed, conceptually speaking, as operations and functions: "a world of parries where the most minute of permutations is supposed to be a response to a new situation or a reply to the indiscreet question ... a transformation of energy..." (Deleuze & Guattari, 1977: 12–13; also Deleuze, 1995: 105). In sum, information and consumption do not elicit natural or stable cultural-political categories at all; to understand the functions of these concepts it is necessary that "each moment of difference must then find its true figure: selection, repetition, ungrounding, the question-problem complex: ... resemblance abolished, the 'disparate' as … unit of measure" (Deleuze, 1994: 68–9). In the next section, my interest is in this disparity – and what it suggests about the use of information and consumption for criticism.

Let me start again then with a discussion of some recent theories that elicit different senses of disparity, theories associated with the writings of Jean-François Lyotard, Gilles Deleuze, and Jean Baudrillard. Following this discussion, I offer some suggestions for using disparities about information and consumption in relation to opportunities and challenges that future cultural-political criticism might consider.

In *The Postmodern Condition*, Lyotard frames information and its consumption around the break or rupture between knowledge and knowers. The strong historical connection between these categories, from the work of the Humboldt's in refashioning German universities to Clark Kerr and the California model of 1960, is said to give way to a new form of knowledge, that of an identity between knowledge and consumers: "The goal is exchange" and "knowledge ceases to be an end in itself, it loses its 'use-value'" (Lyotard, 1979: 4–5). The knower has been de-autonomized – what one knows is only valuable if it adds to the general *translatability* of knowledge. The subject of knowledge is the production of knowledge itself, which will turn out to support emphasis on *mediation* (e.g. teamwork in science, collaboration in art). Lyotard's notion that "we may thus expect a thorough exteriorization of knowledge with respect to the 'knower'" means knowledge is not embodied in human agents and knowledge is dissociable "from the training of minds." Humamachines. It is no longer a question of various territorial powers, governments, parents, and subjects each controlling knowledge in large and small Imperial-style domination over others, whether in occupying a country, a family or a classroom, although they still do, but a question of information having become a "commodity indispensable to productive power … perhaps *the* major-stake in the worldwide competition for power" (Lyotard, 1979: 5). Thus the production and consumption of information sets off competition between maximizing performance and the accumulation of credits – in the arts, old and new criteria of significance are developed to select for canonization, which equals more chances to perform. Chance is grafted to a generalized instability – in the arts and humanities especially, the "best" is quickly contested *and* institutionalized, mostly by falling back on protecting and discrediting prior performances. Information for consumption and consumption of information are not necessarily symmetrical, especially in cultural arenas subject to incessant recontextualization.

In certain areas of knowledge production, author, producer, and consumer can be difficult to distinguish. For example, Mario Biagioli has rigorously examined the "peculiar economy" of scientific production, showing that the proper name of a scientist matters so much because it is not entirely clear where the name "belongs" vis-à-vis attribution: "Scientists can patent useful processes stemming from their research, and yet academic scientific authorship is defined in terms of the truth of scientific claims, not of their possible usefulness in the market ... a scientist qua academic scientist is, literally, a non-author." Knowledge and authors are not symmetrical. Scientific authorship is increasingly valued *and* contested vis-à-vis credit and responsibility: multi-authorship requires concepts of "contributors" and "guarantors," notions that have been proposed to ameliorate contention over how one values the knowledge of the scientist-as-author (Biagioli, 2000: 89, 103ff.).[2] Compare all this to the art-world (*pace* Arthur Danto) where an indirect but vivid discourse can at times sustain the value of the signature (= value). Or is that a myth circulated by artists, part of their desperation-as-artists?

Lyotard and Biagioli are part of a now vast discourse on the consumption of knowledge and information. Issues concerning how to award credit for the construction of useful information in relation to "pure" information opens to *agons* of intellectual property (copyright), to the restrictions placed on *which* differences – thinking, reflecting, doing, testing and the like – may "count" as scientific production, or knowledge production as such. Lyotard insisted that the sheer flow of information draws on many resources, but only if it does not impede "the messages circulating within it [from being] rich in information and easy to decode." Thus, in the biological sciences studies of protein interactions, which go on for years, integrating many other knowledges, goes hand in hand with medical practices that decode symptoms and result in treatments; whereas in the arts and humanities, research commonly turns into the book, which took three or four thousand hours to research and write, but is consumed in a few hours and whose contributions to public or social knowledge remains unknown. The "disparate" element is not to be denied.

The *Postmodern Condition* also outlined the obsolescence of basic relations of knowledge and ignorance: that division – society has to project ignorance (from bad information to ideology to sentimentalism) as a motivation to produce knowledge – gives way to a new dyad, where knowledge is divided between payment and investment, or knowledge that is split into "daily" and "special" codes of consumption. Some of the production of knowledge, or information, about, say, Colonial America passes through specialists, or "decision-makers" who can make judgments about what lasts and doesn't vis-à-vis Colonial American history; other information is consumed as "common" knowledge, the latter "to repay each person's perpetual debt with respect to the social bond." That is, "common" information/knowledge allows for such phrases as "founding fathers" to have a currency – social consumption shaped through social cohesion, while specialists scramble to sustain or find new information (what if Jefferson was a transsexual?). It is worth noting that the fantasy of the definitive fact starts here – in the humanities, the possible *indistinction* between knowledge and, say, anecdote (see Cohen, forthcoming: Chapter 5). Be that as it may, the division of knowledge-as-information into common/special plays out on the political level as well, in the micro-politics of reproduction. The research institution tenures those whose information-knowledge allows the institution to stake out claims of legacy and endowment for the future – there are things (information, interpretations) that must survive. Lyotard took great care to argue that information could be separated off and combined or "packaged" – that it, with consumption, had to negotiate with science (referents) and narrative (social cohesion), themselves apparatuses that sustain institutional internal equilibrium and public conviviality, making it possible for, here, academic "legislators" to have something to legislate.

In general, consumption of information has become structured around rewarding performative utterances, whose "effect on the referent coincides with its enunciation," an icy formula that nonetheless just says that *regulation* of knowledge in any specific system is paramount. Of course there are hybrids: the mixture of comedy TV and political commentary adds to the other once political information has to be processed through humor to reach an audience that expects this — new forms of processing the consumption of consumption. But frequently, information and consumption concern *reproduction* and the avoidance of becoming "noise," unless "noise" is also another type or threshold of information — as in the case of the avant-garde, whose dissonance becomes information and is variously canonized — good consumption for some groups (Lyotard, 1979: 9, 13). The idea, for instance, that this Western avant-garde offers "bad information" (the reception of Cubism, or at least the myth of Cubism's negative reception) that becomes assimilated to the point of canonization, useful as meta-information (as criteria of selection) to evaluate in advance the "destiny" of what comes forward as newly different aesthetic things — is this an addition to a larger indifference? However torqued, access to information is no longer contained by Oedipalizing identifications — the proliferation of new types of information and patterns of consumption (e.g. the extension of branding into micro-behavior) use the dissolution of the grand narratives in order to effectuate new forms of mobile identities *and* new *constraints*. It is not just that communicative functions become inseparable from generalized competition (agonistics), but that maximizing reproduction requires many new supplementary practices. Institutions of all kinds must have constraints that allow for them to protect a future,

> for statements to be declared admissible within its bounds. The constraints function to filter discursive potentials, interrupting potential connections in the communication networks: there are things that should not be said… They also privilege certain classes of statements … there are things that should be said, and there are ways of saying them. (Lyotard, 1979: 17)

Which is to say: information and consumption are processed through numerous axiomatic systems, formal and informal. This presupposes that the production of knowledge has no formula — there are no limits to the processing of information nor to its consumption. "…a process of delegitimation fueled by the demand for legitimation" (Lyotard, 1979: 39). Indeed, "disciplines disappear, overlappings occur at the borders between sciences … an immanent and … 'flat' network of areas of inquiry…" For both science and art, delegitimation can circulate not just as newly capitalized information, but as a "preview" – think of the art review that describes work as "up and coming" or the discourse of "promise" that surrounds scientific investigations, instances where "proof" of value comes not from just performance but the circulation of incorporeal or symbolic value. In any case, information and consumption are less a question of various autonomies of truth than they are the augmentation of power for the future. In the sentence just written, the quotation marks indicate contested practices.

For instance, recent studies suggest that in scientific organizations, information and its consumption cannot be understood just in terms of the effect of practical outcomes or riveted to the ideological goals that discursively tie science to public acceptance. It's rather a question of a conjunction of how and where scientific information is produced. There are different environments – large clinical tests in which portions of the results remain on reserve, some held in private contracts, and there are places such as Fermilab, which runs a continuous tape on its experimental findings, waiting for a "wiggle" to show up that informs as to the necessity of continuation of a test or not. Hyper-information and highly differential consumption are both produced. In addition, the production of knowledge for other scientists is increasingly "magnetized" – the innovation of hypertext in science is giving way to a "semantic web," where electronic publishing adds to meta-data, where keywords as organizers of information are replaced by specific results coded for specific researchers. Research and its publication has to offer a *reserve*, a surplus, not just a result that can be verified or disqualified. The scientist is not just a shuttler between claims over, say, patents and tests and an author-function restricted to making statements that are true of nature (see Biagioli, 2000: 87ff.). Again, think of the highly differential production of information in any new science by comparison to the humanities – nearly all of the recent obituaries of Derrida gleefully dragged deconstruction back to an "origin" in Nazism, an ideological trick of neo-liberalism, neo-marxism, *and* neo-conservatism. Deconstruction's demise returns humanists to "finely grained, empirical research." Or as Stanley Fish put it, catapulted by the *New York Times* to speak for humanists, the promulgation of theory can't help people decide how to live, so we should celebrate the end of theory. I can't recall ever reading a deconstructionist who argued for such implied claims (see Eakin, 2004). Does scientific information increasingly belong to futurology, while the arts/humanities cannot seem to move off *repetition* of one sort or another?

In sum, the *Postmodern Condition* verbalized some new conditions for information and consumption. Gone is the presumption that information "informs" a context shared by all, where, say, an editorial in the *New York Times* makes a decisive intervention in matters of import to the public; instead, it is a question of maintaining the "minimax equilibrium" of pragmatic positions – the *New York Times* must not lose its ability to offer *shares* in what is called public discourse, whether the latter is more imaginary than not. In the cultural sphere, art is not about informing anyone – it is about art as a series of moves that must participate in and add to an increased operativity – the effectivity of, say, a contest between the *authenticity of a present space* and its being turned into spectacle – as heterogeneity is integrated. Bruce Mau, one of the most conspicuous designers now at work in the USA, gives a blunt assessment of this transformation. When asked about the "design revolution" of the past few years in the States, or the ubiquity of "design" as a circulating ideal-form, he insists that "There's a design revolution coming out of North America. It dares to imagine the welfare of the entire human race." When asked what aesthetics should inform design, Mau's response is complete: "The richness of the marketplace." What information is passed on here – what do "welfare," "entire," "human race," and "richness of the marketplace" give to learn, or even to understand (Solomon, 2004)? Is design as articulated here that part of art which refuses to sublimate to the world as it is – yet a sign of aggressive consumability of others and world?[3]

According to the schema laid out in Deleuze and Guattari's *Anti-Oedipus*, the modernist intellectual tended to idealize the scientific and technical worker. This could range from the claims made by Futurists to Marxist theorists (Lukacs) or to any invocation of research as supporting the general "scientificity" of society. The new worker was someone whose genealogy was long and mixed but who could master a flow of information, although such mastery was not distinct from an ultimate, destructive, self-consumption: "so absorbed in capital that the reflux of organized, axiomated stupidity coincides with him, so, that when he goes home in the evening, he rediscovers his little desiring-machines by tinkering with the television set." But even the handyman may well be obsolete once we can just throw our machines away and replace them in a few hours.

For Deleuze and Guattari, information is something different from its graphic representation. Information emerges out of the amorphous continuum of flows and can be attached to any kind of medium, linguistic and not. Only one of its models is the computer: "three million points per second transmitted ... only a few of which are retained ... the computer is a machine for instantaneous and generalized decoding" (Deleuze & Guattari, 1977: 241). More important than its medium, information is a matter of *frequency and redundancy*, and the reference to decoding here means "reciprocal precondition between expression and content for the relationship of subordination between signifier and signified." Information is stripped of any primary identity so that it can both function as figuring sense, mostly common if differentially-coded (image, schema, form of expression), and *be suspended* as needed – timely and untimely, hence stable and unstable. The Western, highly urbanized setting that calls forth the daily newspaper is a place where one consumes up-to-date information but much redundancy; this is a place where readers consume the one-to-many verbalization of homogeneity – phrases related to behaviors that make up the frequency and redundancy of released facts, interpretations, the taking of everyday positions. Information is consumed as part of "the replicative power of the standard norms," and every sub- and even anti-group has its own concentration of the same modes of processing information (see the interesting analysis by De Landa, 1997: 245ff.). In the cultural sphere, a ubiquitous "see (read)-this-now" effect is only one of many timings of information as consumed (Deleuze & Guattari, 1977: 240–5). *A Thousand Plateaus* didn't zero in on information to give a definitive model of it; it set that project aside in favor of talking about *insigning* – the imposition of a messages different sets of coordinates, continuity of power outstripping the communicative: "short phrases that command life and are inseparable from enterprises and large-scale projects. 'Ready'? 'Yes'. 'Go ahead'" (Deleuze & Guattari, 1987: 75–6). Language here is "neither informational nor communication ... not the communication of information but ... the communication of order-words..." Disputes at the Getty Research Center in Los Angeles make for a return to its commanding short phrases: "'Get the greatest and rarest objects,' 'seize the unexpected chance,' 'build on strength,' 'fill gaps, but only with superior examples,' and 'collect collections,'" each a power axiom. (Michnic, 2004) Redundancy is primary – think of the difference between the book review in the *New York Times* that helps to sell 10,000 to 20,000 copies of a heavily promoted book and the prestige value of a low-distributed academic journal, which puts a book up as "indispensable" for the well-educated in a so-called narrow zone of signification – both the indispensable and narrow are obviously contestable political terms because they are redundant in their sphere, their scope and reach. Information and its consumption were conceived by Deleuze and Guattari as traversing one-to-many and many-to-many (Internet, indirect discourse, i.e. "Someone said they heard that someone saw …"), each pulled between repeated acts of redundancy (which is really meta- or super-redundancy), homogenizations (big and small), and those events of demassification, or new attractors for information-making, language as catalyst, where discourse can register new, if small, logics of relation and not a replicating norm. Small areas in the arts and humanities can operate with concepts such as "authentic" communication of a new perspective, but this is more unsettled than ever (De Landa, 1997: 322).

For example, Americans are currently blitzed by the overcoding of information and regimens of consumption about obesity – this latest national health "threat" is being decoded into a social problem, a cultural taboo (it is rare to see an obese curator at an important institution), a politics of consumerism able to punish and reward at the same time. Obesity, information, and consumption thereof, is hardly a single thing to be known or repressed. Indeed, it's part of law (discrimination), psychology, taste, aesthetics, politics, social cohesion, even a Puritan schizo-seme in which obesity is socially common yet imagistically controlled-college catalogues sent out to prospective parents/students are not filled with images of the studious obese. Disseminated through all sorts of media forms, why doesn't obesity then *in-form* as to the nefarious aspects of consumerism-*as-such*, or only does so when channeled into cultural artifacts (*Supersize Me!*)? Is obesity contained by an immanent axiomatic (Deleuze) so that it can be read just as the limit of a good thing (cheap available food)? Does obesity have built-in inoculations against being thought through, so that one can consume obesity-as-poor-consumption, without having to deal with the, so to speak, obesity or enormity of consumerism? To all the indirect, qualitative, and limited codes that regulated the production and consumption of consumer goods, prestige items, women and children in pre-capitalist social formations, full-on capitalism installs specific axiomatics for every point of production, recording and consumption, seen in a monetarization without final code (boundary, limit), and which is in no way separate from an imagification without boundaries (Deleuze & Guattari, 1977: 251). Obesity can be a function of re-hierarchization as much as a liberation of the body from bourgeois norms.

Information and consumption are caught up in decision-making, administration, reaction, inscription. In the rigorous and analytic model offered by Deleuze and Guattari, information and consumption pass into relations of subordination, disjunction, and overcoding. In their model, information and consumption are discernible events and processes, with two constraints: there is an internal axiomatic that regulates, subject to breakdown, combinations of information for consumption, the subject's share or investment in the *Urstatt*, a Statist sense of limit, whether in work, family or culture. And there is an external one, or the actual life of accidents and contingencies. These constraints appear as subordination, which involves, in art, aesthetic processes and products that make object A stand in for other expressive series. Subordination is not, ironically, separate from disjunction, which calls forth practices that rebuild hierarchies, as in the emergence of architecture as a meta-discourse for art and science, at least in certain dimensions (the grafting of tourism to site to building to institution to objects). Overcoding brings with it an emphasis on practices that veer toward contextual controls of the contemporary (Deleuze & Guattari, 1977: 262). Those Lyotardian artists and intellectuals of the postmodern – experimenters in the construal of the sublime – know overcoding all too well, a line of continuation to what Adorno and Horkheimer called the "culture-industry." In particular, overcoding is active in tactics where negative integration and negative exclusion pass into the other. Consider the way the revival of an institution is cast by its managers – the resurgence of the Hammer Museum in Los Angeles is spoken of in terms that could have been written by Adorno and Horkheimer, its aesthetic standards said to be based on "consumer's needs," so as to better control "any trace of spontaneity from the public," in whose name one represents:

> At the same time that this incredible art scene was developing in Los Angeles with all these young artists coming out of school ... there wasn't an institution that was taking care of them. The galleries were carrying most of the burden of showing what was happening. We stepped into that void. (Sheets, 2004)

On one level, this communicates the obvious; on another, one could ask why art is spoken as having "burdens" and "voids," or guilt and emptiness? What is communicated as information there?

Finally, consider another strong perspective on information and consumption. Have we really understood what Baudrillard has argued in this conceptual arena? Baudrillard is among the most interesting post-historicists of the group around "French Theory," that intellectual and critical formation which suspended loss, lack, negation as the defining characteristics of modern life, setting them aside because so marked by an indefensible abuse of historicity and control of institutions (see Lotringer & Cohen, 2001).

Simulations was offered as counter-ethnology, since the post World War II reinvigoration of social theory had turned into, for Baudrillard, the re-injection of "fictional differences everywhere." The juggernaut of information and consumption is intrinsic to the "magnetic field" of simulation. Simulation was defined as "a precession of the model" – reality transformed so as to make *reversibility* impossible, or capital's unique ability to cancel history – as in newly sanctioned ideologies, or the runaway competition of new groups around economy, society, and culture. Simulation is able to effect a "short-circuit" of facts and events so as to extract value from mostly political and power-tripping *conjunctures* (Baudrillard, 1983: 32–4). Simulation is isomorphic with consumer society to the extent that simulation, like consumer society, "is its own purpose and so is self-propelling..." as it is constituted on the "*impossibility of gratification and measures its progress by ever-rising demand*" (see the remarks by Bauman, 2001: 13). Or, as Deleuze and Guattari put it, capitalist schizophrenia. Hence, simulation is threaded to consumer society – in both, there is perpetual destruction of the real for the more than real, the true stake. The more insecurity that runs through specific channels of a social system, the more opportunity of joining human wish and social order: a "policy of precarization" in which irrationality is consumed just like any other thing (Bauman, 2001: 18). As the structural logic of need gave way to, first, desire and then to sheer wish as the driving process of consumer society, for Baudrillard it is aggression that energizes contemporary social systems, including information and consumption. More resources than ever are devoted to compete for admission to the best schools, while discourses of crisis and desire over schooling mix with the other. Competitive behavior is grafted to information – how to succeed in getting in – processed by a differential logic of institutional, aggressive exclusion, in no way separate from the consumption of information. In the past year in, again, Los Angeles, two of its premier venues – the Los Angeles County Museum of Art and the Los Angeles Museum of Contemporary Art – offered surveys of Minimalist works, each said to be four to six years in the assembling of the artifacts, including the catalogue essays. Where are the effects of such prodigious condensations of information? What were the actual goals of the show and how are they different from their *sign-goals*, that is, the consequences of their *mode of presentation* (a museum, curators, collectors, reviewers, use in schools, commerce, didacticism, etc.)? My own discourse implies motivation by the institutions in marshaling their resources – but what is that implication actually worth if it is another simulation – the critics – where criticism finds something to pin a problem on? Am I just recoding the formula that information plus consumption plus simulation = reproduction? Yet, information and consumption do pass into hyper-information and hyper-consumption, almost imperceptibly, or incorporeally – a con[-]fusion between goal and sign-goal, here between the show to represent history and the show to represent the institutions and its workers making history significant; where is the real (is it consumed by its material effects)? Such events congeal in another dimension, the mixture of sign and goal an "indefinite refraction" of event, process, outcome, sign, reproduction, where archaic and despotic codes – wooing the collector and deciding on things to be seen – are set within new codes of radical corporate depersonalization, both part of a reserve cultural capital, but even that designation is a bit rigid.

For Baudrillard, scientific information and consumption, like all the other types of information and consumption, moves to that "objective irony of things caught in their own devices – no longer the historical workings of the negative, but the workings of reduplication and the rising stakes ... delirious contiguity ... pure 'objectality'" (Baudrillard, 1987: 83). In his admirable *Theory Death of the Avant-Garde*, Paul Mann called this objectifying irony the dematerialization of the apparatus, or exposure of the real and its fictions, adding to the fusion of the incredulity/reality of culture and society. For Baudrillard, many intellectuals and artists, caught up in resistance to bad information and mal-consumption (misrepresentation), which, since Baudelaire at least, join in the politics of representing art as avant-garde, are nonetheless oblivious to the larger indifference that also belongs to information and consumption. After over a hundred years of the avant-garde at war with itself and other groups, "the masses plunge into an ecstatic indifference ... [they] use information in order to disappear; information uses the masses as shroud – a marvelous ruse of our history..." If the avant-garde didn't have the academy and sectors of the gallery world to rely upon for its basic platform, what would it have? Who speaks for whom? Who is the new and better subject of desire, especially once visibility is the stake of cultural stakes – once alienation and spectacle is replaced by the immediate transparency of what *can be*, set within the "raw and inexorable light of information and communication" one of the ways processes of indifference work (Baudrillard, 1987: 89–95)? When objective irony is the subject, what to make of our political-cultural life? The hundreds of millions of dollars spent by the Kerry and Bush campaigns, in whatever form, is devoted to swaying a tiny percentage of the population to go one way and not another – it adds to the larger indifference of what it takes to reduce politics to "to-win." In another realm of cultural life, a review of an academic book in a hip-quasi-academic magazine like *Artforum's BookForum* may well enhance the sensibility that art and scholarship are not riddled by unbridgeable differences. The art, scholarly, reviewing zones meet, for instance, over "noir," that subject said to fascinate across cultural zones (or most often, pets and Nazis, according to a reviewer in the *New York Times*). But why review when the reviewer can only quote the author: "The film noir cycle should ... be understood as a compensatory response to the actual disappearance of older urban forms," that is, noir was the castration complex as culture (Polito, 2004). Noir is excellent sublimation to tell us about loss. Does anyone believe that making visible a text on films cast as "compensations" for what perhaps no one ever experienced is a vital cultural phenomenon? At what cost, this consumption of culture as melancholy?

Simulations argued that the "law of supply and demand" had supplanted every other social bond – only production and mass consumption still had a tenuous hold on earlier formations of the real (Baudrillard, 1983: 46). The critical hypothesis here concerns the shift from ideology to scenario: piece by piece, life as scenario brings a "wizardry" of work, society, production, consumption, culture, self, the "mortal blows of simulation," or those "inmixture[s]" of all mediums and all messages, a

> viral, endemic, chronic, alarming presence of the medium without our being able to isolate its effects, spectralized, like those publicity holograms sculptured in empty space with laser beams, the event filtered by the medium – the dissolution of TV into life, the dissolution of life into TV – an indiscernible chemical solution … [an] induction … infiltration … illegible violence … an IMPLOSION (Baudrillard, 1983: 54–7).

As an example, watch non-Philistine literature burn in America: the recent decision and announcement by the American National Book Award committee had five finalists in fiction, all unknown, with poor sales by commercial standards. The committee did its job of finding books to read that had something to say about literature's form of expression and variable relations with the milieu; they were chastised not simply by the Philistines for perpetuating an elitist sense of writing, but by the publishers who insisted that such a prestigious award committee ought to promptly get in touch with the American people. "It is not clear that literature benefits when one of its signal awards involves only books read by a few hundred people" (Wyatt, 2004). Are readers still "readers" when books offer little actual challenge?

As the example/event concerning the National Book Awards suggests, information and consumption, at least with high-end smart-prize culture, connects with something disparate – the effect of smart literature and few readers, the latter the content or the information. Are there shares of disparity to be distributed, since it cannot be denied that smart-literature is one of many hundreds of markets in the consumption of literature, and every market has its disjunctions? Do the Book Awards announce relief in abandoning a cultural tension between the smart-about-literature and the many, at least on the part of publishers?

The writings discussed above are about choices, including poor ones, and multiple disjunctions enacted across universities, professors, artists, professional critics, and artifacts – places, roles, and things to be seen and discussed. Choice is intrinsic to cultural expectations and demands. It is attendant on class and psycho-political selections, an idea from Margaret Mead, taken up by Claude Lévi-Strauss, who pushed to the threshold where information and its consumption leads to the organized disintegration of culture:[5]

> Every verbal exchange, every line printed, establishes communication between people, thus creating an evenness of level, where before there was an information gap and consequently a greater degree of organization. (Lévi-Strauss, 1978: 414)

Lévi-Strauss postulated a gap in information which implies a gap in the consumption of information; this relation stands in for motivation in the daily life of contemporary capitalism – knowledge in art and science is driven by the at once means/goal of closing gaps. Science closes them by, say, war on disease, while the arts close the gap between contemporary life and the shedding of older sensibilities, art practices frequently an overcoding set within *recoding*. Other questions are exposed: do super-capitalized societies or at least the cultural and political sectors within them disintegrate once information is capitalized to the point of extreme differentiation – and do new integrations of differences add to larger disjunctions? The instance of the National Book Awards suggests that the game (operation, function, simulation) of making new, vital, literature *notable* contests the game of making literature marketable – where individuation and homogenization, taken together, make it difficult for individuation to exist *outside* homogenization.

This has become particularly acute not just in science, where assigning credit is difficult, but in the arts, where artists now hang on the visible review or institutional reproduction (position) that has come to stand in for public significance.

Consumption in an Age of Information concerns choices and disjunctions that derive from such culturally incorporative practices as neo-canonization, with its current ability to integrate and exclude at once. Scientific and artistic practices congeal in centers that collect information – all the major museums and universities compete in the market for aesthetic and other things that testify to chances to continue to compete in the future. The scientific and artistic multi-centers of knowledge are as much markets for investors and new types of investments as they are "trainers" of skill. The overall labor devoted to making contemporary culture notable and memorable also increases the value of specific information about it – the right review at the right time, which holds for all political groupings, "right" having become a synecdoche of social life. Writers such as Bauman are probably correct to insist that the ability to colonize new wishes of a specific population gives information and consumption unbounded categorical relations. The French theorists discussed above all stressed information and consumption are not bound by any code.

In the genealogy of information and consumption, there is one track (ready, steady, go!) that starts with Kant's arguments for a "spontaneous subject," a subject who can make autonomy into a process and a goal, who can give rules to experience neither out of suffering nor hedonistic indulgence. That meant good choices, or information and its consumption subsumed to practical ends that are differently welded to common goals. But in a social regime that is organized around preventing further disjunction as it actually intensifies disparities, what is the value of autonomy in relation to selection processes? Who gives autonomy? What gives autonomy? How do universities – "smart" choosers – decide to invest in, say, contemporary art in relation to other selections made and not made? Imbroglios here move from university-based cultural systems, whose language is at odds with commercial venues, but not its practices ("star" a value to both), to the staggering indifference education plays in the organization of public life in the USA. If we turn to literary-based cultures, who and what makes up the "reading public," a phrase coined by Coleridge? If we ask about art, who or what makes up the audience for contemporary art and what does the notion of audience really mean (Bygrave, 2000: 6ff.)? Does this "public" choose, or is it more a mythic public subject? Catalogues and books for the canonic high-end market are quite expensive; but do we think catalogues and books celebrating and promoting new art are different because new? Listen to one of the sharper curators of the contemporary scene, for whom the disparity between art and capital is everywhere and nowhere:

> When Gabriel Orozco puts an orange on the stalls of a deserted brazilian market or slings a hammock in the MoMA garden, he is operating at the hub of "social infra-thinness" (*l'inframince social*), that minute space of daily gestures determined by the superstructure made up of "big" exchanges, and defined by it... The exhibition is the special place where such momentary groupings may occur... (Bourriaud, 2002: 17–18)

Art will be made and consumed through the activation of disparity so as to exploit the whole of space – here is one of the places where disparity and desperation meet. Another example: the *New York Review of Books* recently had an essay on the Walt Disney Concert Hall in Los Angeles, calling it "...the acropolis LA has been waiting for." How does this breathtakingly inept historical comparison – where are the slaves and virgins? – fit with the architect of the hall whose discourse veers toward the personal and emotional (Filler, 2003a, 2003b)? This $US 275 million building now "in-forms" various images for different groups in LA, but which means that the administration of visible high-culture is confused with cultural importance, which is hardly new. Roland Barthes took up these issues nearly fifty years ago, and one might have thought that awareness of mythology, an ur-form of the ways in which political-economic discourse is consumed, involving devices of rhetoric such as *omission*, would be "first nature" for criticism by artists and intellectuals. This is not the case. When individuals enter the "public"– things displayed, an arena for rivalrous claims, trading zones, like that of reputation – each person must now be polite, to the point of ruining an actual exchange between audience and speaker. In the public realm, consumption is often cut free from information, in more than one way.[6] Baudrillard's warnings about simulation seem like basic common sense for a contemporary cultural analyst. Are public venues the place where such "good" bad faith is invited, even required (Hartley, 2000: 71ff.)?

Disparity between public life and individual judgment, or between publicness as confirmation of itself and an individual's alienation (Knowledge? Irony?) is where criticism opens some space for thought. I am suggesting that we think of information and consumption in the cultural sphere through its disjunctions, those strong levers that offer angles of engagement with data, affects, beliefs, practices. Certainly, exploiting disjunctions has the effect of *lessening* the space between our descriptions, ideals and practices. Can criticism become dangerous vis-à-vis myth consumption – those words that incoherently summon order and value (Barthes, 1972: 156; Hacking, 1999: 21)? Criticism today might be this movement where opening and lessening are joined – raising the ante on the coherence of what is said (information) and shown (consumed), defamiliarizing the existing investments, but most of all asking about the politics of culture. This kind of criticism works with disparities not to denounce them from some lofty ideal, but to engage them: to conceive the processes that produce even the consumption of incoherence. As I understand such things, the job of an intellectual (critic, citizen) working in a mode of criticism is to *add another perspective* – to bring the stakes forward. For instance, is "public life" – as ordinarily conveyed by, say, a book-review – actually "public"? A recent review in the *New York Times* of a high-middlebrow book on Benjamin Franklin locates this book within "…the best of the recent biographies [of the Founding Fathers] … a flair for finding flaws within greatness" (Ellis, 2003: 11). Is the implied audience for this book then to be conceived as "connoisseurs" of "flaws," which makes the "great" of "greatness" more secure because flawed? Is this knowledge for the democratic myth that high and low are not so distant from the other, in which case it is a simulation, homogenization and simple coding of a mythed social origin, a trace of some grand narrative Lyotard insisted had cracked-up?

Many of these topics require more interpretation and explanation, not less – less being one of the characteristics of contemporary critical writing. When Lyotard offers there are no limits to the production of knowledge as the actual subject of the social, or when Deleuze and Guattari speak to the no boundaries of monetarization, or Baudrillard takes us to the "objective irony" of our system(s), then, I think, the critic might start with a sense of language-trouble. Here one suspends belief in "normal language" – the kinds of euphemism and politeness ordinarily encountered in universities – and equally keeps distance from the discourses that urge on us the next new thing. In both cases, it is ineffectual for criticism to start with any "safe" notion of language, especially the idea that one is going to find some bedrock of fact, concept or principle which makes language continuous with representation or that synthesizes information and consumption. It is better to conceive language in terms of divergences and decenterings that undercut representation. It is better to conceive of language *at the outset* as a mixed-system, reference on one side, folk-wisdom (*pace* the philosopher Arthur Danto) or collective "common sense" on the other, the actual and virtual at once, with unresolvable problems of literalism, problems of delirium, problems of making meaning always *mean*. An ongoing issue here is how to offer concepts to make a plausible "picture" of the context that allows one to "read" the present.

Finally, the credibility of representing a public – reliance on trustworthy information – is an underlying membrane of public life and criticism today, which stretches across our institutions, our visible public intellectuals, our common references to a culture that is somehow meant to include all of us. But our current amalgam of public culture requires the elimination of danger, risk, and nuanced doubt from *public language;* we increasingly live out what one writer calls a situation of circulating impossible ideals set amidst the furious maximization of individuation – of memory, of subject, of art, school, text, others – everything (Mann, 1999). Nearly fifteen years ago, in a highly publicized (and expensive) volume, *Out There: Marginalization and Contemporary Cultures,* Cornel West called for a criticism that would be *demystifying* and *prophetic* at once, the two terms joined to a "new cultural politics of difference," or inclusion of neglected groups and experiences. A criticism that "affirms the perennial quest for the precious ideals of individuality and democracy…" where even "one's soul" was at stake (West, 1990: 31). To focus on disparity in different spheres of information and consumption is at best *demythifying*, not demystifying; one wants to make critical discourse hard to consume but active in its applications – is this an invocation of a new "distressed subject," a writer-reader who does not forget that "public life" is a curious and highly politicized arena in which it is hard to tell "public" from phantom? And is anything but prophetic.

NOTES

1. My approach to information and consumption is akin to Avital Ronell's *Stupidity* (2002), where she offered that the contemporary intellectual and artist ought not to go to war over stupidity. Intellectuals and artists should elicit melancholy from one's experiences of the stupid-is-as-stupid-does. The thoughtful, reflective writer conveys, according to Ronell, the "crushing blow that comes from someone or something … exceeding your grasp. The matter of receiving the blow is already beyond your capacity to understand … not much else to do but dumbly go on, you can't go on." That is certainly an allegory of cultural production in the USA, one that freely circulates especially around Unversity conduits, a new version of the "unhappy consciousness" of the professorate and professional artists. Ronell cuts-out a position complementary with Derrida's demand in *Specters of Marx* (1994) for an enthusiastic "new scholar" who can speak to being-haunted, who can take up the challenge of not-going-to-war-against the past, Derrida's injunction forwarding the new information of a messianic Marxism no longer threaded to class-warfare. In the case of both stupidity and being-haunted, neither can be defeated and, for both writers being stupid and haunted meets its match with history itself, no less, "diminished to the raw grappling – the solitary warfare – of a distressed subject." What then is the subject of this "distressed subject"? For whom? To be consumed how?

2. Thanks to Mario Biagioli for a discussion on scientific knowledge production.

3. I'm not particularly inclined to psychoanalysis, but Geza Roheim's comments about culture and sublimation seem to fit some of the

extravagant and extroverted discourse that runs through the claims for design (Roheim, 1971: 122ff.).

4. The title of the article from the *New York Times* says its all: "Armand Hammer's Orphan Museum Turns Into Cinderella in Los Angeles" (Sheets, 2004).

5. Thanks to Tom Lutz for a discussion on this section.

6. For example, I attended a reading last year at the *Los Angeles County Museum of Art* by an author known in Southern California as an early champion of conceptual poetry; but it was the third time that I heard the same talk – I could have informed the speaker that I thought he was assuming the audience's innocence, but instead I just "ate" my boredom. Who was the talk for if not the innocent consumer, that is, subjects ready for myth?

REFERENCES

Barthes, Roland (1972), *Mythologies*. New York: Hill and Wang.

Baudrillard, Jean (1983), *Simulations*. New York: Semiotext(e).

—— (1987), *Ecstasy of Communication*. New York: Semiotext(e).

Bauman, Zygmunt (2001), "Consuming Life," *Journal of Consumer Culture* I (I): 9–29.

Biagioli, Mario (2000), "Rights or Rewards? Changing Contexts and Definitions of Scientific Authorship," *Journal of College and University Law* 27 (I): 83–108.

Bourriaud, Nicolas (2002), *Relational Aesthetics*. Dijon: Les presses du reel.

Bygrave, Stephen (2000), "'And Art Thou Nothing?': Dialogue and Critique in Romanticism," *New Formations*, No. 41: 5–20.

Cohen, Sande (forthcoming), *History Out of Joint: Essays on the Use and Abuse of History*. Baltimore, Johns Hopkins University Press.

Manuel De Landa, *A Thousand Years of Non-Linear History*. New York: Zone Books, 1997.

Deleuze, Gilles (1994), *Difference and Repetition*. New York: Athlone.

—— (1995), *Bergsonism*. New York: Zone Books.

—— and Felix Guattari (1977), *Anti-Oedipus*. Minneapolis: University of Minnesota Press.

—— and Felix Guattari (1987), *A Thousand Plateaus*. Minneapolis: University of Minnesota Press.

Dennis, Dion (2003), "The Digital Death Rattle of the American Middle Class: A Cautionary Tale," *Ctheory*, 26 (3); http://www.ctheory.net.

Derrida, Jacques (1994), *Specters of Marx*. London: Routledge.

Eakin, Emily (2004), "The Theory of Everything, R.I.P.," *New York Times*, October 17, 2004, p. 12.

Ellis, Joseph J. (2003), "The Many-Minded Man," *New York Times*, July 6, p. 11.

Filler, Martin (2003a), "Towering Vision," *New York Times Magazine*, January 5, 2003, p. 15.

—— (2003b), "Victory at Bunker Hill," *New York Review of Books*, October 23, p. 55.

Genette, Gerard (1995), *Mimologics*. Lincoln and London: University of Nebraska Press.

Hacking, Ian (1999), *The Social Construction of What?* Cambridge, MA: Harvard University Press.

Hartley, John (2000), "Conflict Not Conversation: The Defeat of Dialogue in Bakhtin and de Man," *New Formations*, No. 41: 71–82.

Horkheimer, Max and Theodor W. Adorno (1972), *The Dialectic of Enlightenment*. New York: Herder and Herder.

Lévi-Strauss, Claude (1978), *Tristes Tropiques*. New York: Atheneum.

Lotringer, Sylvère and Sande Cohen (2001), "Introduction," *French Theory in America*. New York: Routledge.

Lyotard, Jean-François (1979), *The Postmodern Condition*. Minneapolis: University of Minnesota Press.

Mann, Paul (1999). *Masocriticism*. Albany: State University of New York Press.

McSherry, Corynne (2001), *Who Owns Academic Work?* Cambridge, MA: Harvard University Press.

Michnic, Suzanne (2004), "Crossroads on Getty Hill," *Los Angeles Times*, November 8, p. E4.

Parisi, Luciana (2004), *Abstract Sex*. London: Continuum.

Pinker, Stephen (1997), *How the Mind Works*. New York: Norton.

Polito, Robert (2004), "Noir Space," *Bookforum*, Oct/Nov, p. 38.

Roheim, Geza (1971) *The Origin and Function of Culture*. New York: Anchor.

Ronell, Avital (2002), *Stupidity*. Urbana and Chicago: University of Illinois Press.

Sheets, Hilarie M. (2004), "Armand Hammer's Orphan Museum Turns Into Cinderella in Los Angeles," *New York Times*, October 6, Arts, p. 1.

Solomon, Deborah (2004), "Designs for Living," *Los Angeles Times Magazine*, September 26, p. 17.

Strathern, Marilyn (2000), "Afterword: accountability ... and ethnography," in Marilyn Strathern (ed.), *Audit Cultures*. London: Routledge, pp. 279–97.

West, Cornel (1990), "The New Cultural Politics of Difference," in R. Ferguson, M. Gever, Trinh T. Minh-Ha, and Cornel West (eds), *Out There: Marginalization and Contemporary Cultures*, Cambridge, MA: MIT Press, pp. 19–38.

Wyatt, Edward (2004), "New Novels, Big Awards, No Readers," *New York Times Week in Review*, October 17, p. 12.

Index